Sept '81.

To louise·· —
May your pen never
RUN dRU —— With
Much love é' Best wishes,
KRIS— Dina é' THE POD
.XXX.

Sidney Sime

S.H.SIME

Simon Heneage and Henry Ford

Sidney Sime

Master of the Mysterious

with 84 illustrations

THAMES AND HUDSON

Frontispiece Sidney Sime, photographed by E. O. Hoppé
in 1911

Printed in Great Britain by BAS Printers Limited,
Over Wallop, Hampshire
Bound in Great Britain

Contents

Acknowledgments

We would like to thank the sons of three of Sidney Sime's closest associates, Lord Dunsany, Lord Howard de Walden and Gwydion Brooke, for their kindness and help. Many others have been helpful in various ways, especially Mark Amory, Lord Gowrie, Michael Hurd, Bridget Lakin, Lionel Lambourne, B. Y. McPeake, Susan Moore, Colin Morris, Roger Parris, Fiddes Watt and the Secretary of the Federation of British Artists. We would also like to thank members of the Langham Sketching Club, Christine Buchanan, of the Liverpool Record Office, the staff of the Chelsea Reference Library and the Manchester Central Reference Library.

We wish to record our appreciation of the assistance rendered by John Sime and Mrs Stevens, nephew and niece of Sidney Sime, Adrian Beach ARCA, Mr Heather, caretaker of the Worplesdon Memorial Hall, Miss Gabriel and Mrs Wadey, inhabitants of Worplesdon, and we are very grateful to Mrs Grenyer and the other trustees of the Sime Memorial Gallery; in particular, we are indebted to them for granting permission to quote from an unpublished typescript on the work of S. H. Sime, written in 1948 by the author and illustrator, James Thorpe. Unless otherwise attributed the quotations ascribed to him refer to this source.

S.H. and H.F.

Caricature of Sidney Sime by Max Beerbohm for the *Idler*, 1900

Illustration credits

Illustrated London News, pp. 18 and 20; Hoppé, frontispiece; Potter Books Ltd, pp. 12, 13 (top), 15 and 41; Victoria and Albert Museum, London, pp. 16 (both) and 19.

Introduction

'It must be wonderful, Sime, to look like nothing else on earth', remarked Max Beerbohm, and the caricature he drew of Sidney Sime for the *Idler*, August 1900, made him look like an oriental wizard in a bearskin.

Everything about Sime was extraordinary: his appearance, his personality, his life and his art. In *Confessions of an Incurable Collector*, Desmond Coke, the novelist, talked of Sime's 'overwhelming presence as of a chunky Chinese idol'. Perhaps the best description of Sime came in Frank Harris's *Contemporary Portraits*:

a strongly built man of about five feet seven or eight with a cliff-like, overhanging, tyrannous forehead. His eyes are superlative, greyish blue looking out under heavy brows, eyes with a pathetic patience in them as of one who has lived with sorrow; and realizes – "the weary weight of all this unintelligible world." From time to time humorous gleams light up the eyes and the whole face; mirth on melancholy – a modern combination.

All accounts agree on the strength and originality of Sime's character. Some saw him as a poet, some as a philosopher, others as a humorist; Lady Dunsany, in a letter to his widow, described him simply as 'a marvellous talker'. She had seen him hold his own with 'A.E.' and recounted this episode with H. G. Wells:

When Sime and Wells really got going it was a joy to listen. S was out for blood and when W in illustrating a point said 'You and I know we shall die', S interposed 'I don't know it.' He did not admit death, generally accepted truths, or the necessary limitations and conventions of language as premises to argue from.

Sime's letters also give evidence of a man with no respect for conventions or accepted opinion.

He started as a pit-boy, became a celebrity in the Nineties, collaborated with and became a close friend of two talented noblemen, and died poor and forgotten. Sime's life reads like a popular Victorian novel.

His extraordinary art attracted much praise – 'a poet of rare and exquisite genius', said the art critic Haldane Macfall, while Hannen Swaffer, the journalist, called him 'the greatest imaginative English artist since Blake'. Yet even his admirers did not find it easy to categorize Sime's art: often they took refuge in the wish to see it again. 'I hope before long he will give us a collection of his drawings', said the essayist and poet Richard Le Gallienne as early as 1899. 'I speak only as a layman but I know one or two critics of authority who would welcome the opportunity of saying what they think of his remarkable gift.' Similar requests followed. 'One day I hope he will publish his drawings in volume form and so consolidate his position as a great master of the grotesque', wrote Walter Emanuel, the artist and critic, in the *Strand Magazine*, November 1915, while the magazine *Apollo*, reviewing his 1927 exhibition, declared, 'His drawings and caricatures clamour for publication in book form.' The last to echo Le Gallienne was Gordon Ray in *The Illustrator and the Book in England 1790–1914*. Ray wrote:

Of all English black-and-white artists more or less in the Beardsley tradition, he [Sime] was the most original. If his designs were collected and republished they might well turn out to be more impressive than those of Edmund Dulac or Kay Nielsen despite the advantage those artists gained from working in colour.

The best of Sime's work is in this book and much of it, reproduced from the original drawings and printed with modern expertise, has renewed impact. Of its power there can be no doubt. About its nature there may still be argument. Sime himself declared that he had 'an inherent bent towards mystery' and he was always at pains to make his pictures more mysterious. Probably Lord Dunsany got closer to the truth than anyone. He said that his own writing was 'guided by two lights that do not seem very often to shine together, poetry and humour', and he thought of Sime's art, which he admired passionately, in much the same way. In an article in the *Fortnightly Review* published in August 1942, the year after Sime's death, he drew attention to the commonplace objects in Sime's pictures which remind us of reality: 'stovepipes'; 'the little iron clamp in "cliffs too vast for our world"'; 'the man with the scrubbing brush and bucket'. 'His pictures give us the feeling', wrote Dunsany, 'that, however terrible things may seem in this world or among the asteroids, they are really rather a joke.'

The Early Years

Sidney Sime was born in the Hulme district of Manchester, second of six children, whose parents were David and Helen Sime, both Scottish. The exact date of his birth is uncertain but, according to his nephew John Sime, it was most probably 1865.*

*Two standard dictionaries of artists give the date as 1867, but a birth certificate was not a legal requirement at the time and Sime left no will. In the letter of administration taken out by his widow and his brother after his death on 22 May 1941 his age was given as seventy-six, suggesting that he was born in 1864 or 1865.

Sidney at one time 'did a bit of research' into the history of the family and gave up, he said, when he 'got as far as a drunken cattle-drover in Inverness'.

There are conflicting accounts of his early life. Sime himself told the *Liverpool Echo* in 1927, 'I was quite a youngster when the family left for Liverpool. My father was employed in a furniture warehouse, and as soon as I was old enough I began work.' There would have been little, if any, formal education for the young Sime family, and this lack must have acted as a spur to Sidney who took pains to educate himself throughout his life.

At one time Sime worked as a pit-boy in a Yorkshire colliery. It may have been his first job. The discomfort and occasional horrors of this time are vividly described by Sime in an interview with Arthur Lawrence for the *Idler*, January 1898. 'You know that when the coal has been taken out of the seam it is shovelled into what are called scoops, holding about 5 cwt. My duty, as one of the boys employed for that work, was to push this scoop along the rails to an endless chain, by which it was carried to the pit's mouth and pulled up to the surface.' He went on to say, 'The tunnel through which we had to pull the trolley was only 28 or 30 inches high, and so we had to run along with the body bent at right angles, and if you straightened yourself up at all, the consequences were rather unpleasant.' This existence went on for about five years, Sime told Lawrence.

The word 'pit' has a netherworldly ring to it; miners had their own folklore and 'familiars': goblins, Coblynau, Cutty Soams, Dunters and Knockers, who were bringers of or defenders from the ever-present dangers. Thorpe writes that Sime used to scratch drawings of imps and devils on the walls of the pit. Sime told Lawrence that he had been fond of doing little things – which he called sketches – whenever he could find a moment.

But these moments were to remain few. Sime worked long hours and the late evening was the only time he had for 'work'. Together with a 'musician friend', Crichton Mackay, he would go out 'armed with a bull's-eye lantern and my paint-box, on the lookout for moonscapes. One night I got hold of what seemed to me a good subject and I painted the village church in the early morning by sunrise. . . . Mackay would occasionally bring his guitar; we used to quote all the poetry we could remember, and felt we were going in for genuine romance.' He had a patron at the time. 'An estimable plumber' bought his 'Church at Sunrise' for twenty shillings.

Besides working in the pits, he did other jobs. Accounts of these vary, but they apparently included working for a linen-draper in Lancashire and as an assistant to a baker and a shoemaker. Arthur Lawrence records 'a brief experience with a barber, he did the shaving and I did the lathering. After that I went in for sign-writing,' Sime told Lawrence, 'and I did so well with this that I started on my own account and so found sufficient time and energy to join the Liverpool School of Art.'

The first hard facts about Sime's life emerge from the records of the Liverpool School of Art. This establishment had grown out of the Institute High School for Boys, founded and financed by the Holt ship-owning family, and occupied part of the same building. In the Eighties it was part of a national network of art schools stretching out from South Kensington.

The first relevant entry in the school's records shows that Sime was awarded the full second grade certificate of the Department of Science and Art, South Kensington, in 1885. This would indicate that, if he had undertaken the normal course, he would have begun his studies for the first grade in 1883.

In 1885 his 'free-hand drawing' and 'model drawing' were considered 'excellent' and he won a prize for each; he passed in 'perspective'. He got his third grade certificate in 1886, with a particular commendation for drawing 'from the antique'. In the National Competition in 1888, he was awarded a bronze medal for life-drawing from South Kensington, a silver medal and books for life-drawing by the directors of the Liverpool Institute, and the McDiarmid Prize for the best work from the Liverpool School of Art submitted for this competition.

During this period Sime was in the habit of visiting the Walker Art Gallery and copied, among other paintings, 'Dante's Dream' by Rossetti. The gallery held annual autumn exhibitions, which were the northern equivalent of the Royal Academy Summer Exhibition. Sime's portrait of Henry Peet, Esq., appeared there in 1889. It was his first exhibited picture and was not for sale.

Having completed his studies, Sime had to face the problem of how to earn his living as an artist. He could teach, paint portraits or draw illustrations. Sime chose the third course. 'After a while I realised that the only profitable life for a beginner was book illustrating,' he said to the *Liverpool Echo*. Inevitably he gravitated towards London.

The Magazines

Although working as an illustrator did not at first turn out to be the 'profitable' life that Sime had anticipated, the forces of change were on his side. The use of photography was on the increase in the 1880s while the art of wood-engraving was in decline. Revolutionary new methods of reproducing artwork by mechanical means, using 'process-engraving' in line or half-tone, were coming into general use. This new technology greatly reduced the cost of printing illustrated magazines which grew in number as a result. For artists, especially for those who worked in black-and-white, this was a welcome development since it meant that demand for their work increased, and also that they could experiment in the new techniques and be more certain of achieving the effects they desired. But the limitations of 'process' had to be understood. Aubrey Beardsley and Phil May, most of whose work was done in pen and ink, used it triumphantly; the drawings of those artists who relied on wash or a mixture of media sometimes suffered disastrously. In general, however, the introduction of process-engraving was a blessing to illustrators and the 1890s witnessed a renaissance of an art that had been declining since the great days of the Sixties when artists like Millais, Sandys, Keene, Walker, Pinwell and Boyd Houghton were at their peak.

* * *

What a variety of well-illustrated magazines there was! For the frivolous there were *Pick-Me-Up* and *Ally Sloper's Half Holiday*, and for the less frivolous there were the *Pall Mall Magazine*, the *Idler* and the *English Illustrated Magazine*. For the pious there were the *Quiver* and *Good Words*. For those interested in current affairs and the social scene there were the *Illustrated London News*, the *Graphic* and the *Sketch*. For children there were the *Boy's Own Paper*, *Chums* and *Little Folks*. For lower-middle-brows there were the *Strand Magazine* and its imitators, the *Windsor Magazine* and *Pearson's*. And, of course, there was *Punch*.

But the periodicals we now think of as most typical of the Nineties are the ones that would have appealed to Dorian Gray rather than Mr Pooter, those with a flavour of the *fin de siècle* like the *Yellow Book* and the *Savoy*. 'One *Pick-Me-Up* artist, and only one, had anything approaching *fin de siècle* tendencies', wrote Holbrook Jackson in *The Eighteen Nineties*; 'that artist was (and is) S. H. Sime; he is an art product of the Nineties along with Aubrey Beardsley, Charles Conder, Charles Ricketts and Laurence Housman.'

Sime contributed five full-page illustrations to *Pick-Me-Up* during 1895 and they created an instant sensation. They dealt with the predicaments of 'Ye Shades' in the after-life from a humorous, sometimes satirical, point of view. The settings were often eerie and the humour grim. They gave a boost to the circulation of *Pick-Me-Up*; and they made Sime's name.

Pick-Me-Up, starting in 1888 and selling for a penny, was subtitled 'A Literary and Artistic Tonic for the Mind'. The mind to be revitalized was not the most thoughtful, to judge by the level of the text, but the artwork was another matter. 'I should like you to send me *Pick-Me-Up* every week – it is a dreadfully amusing paper – never fails to make me almost yell', says a character in Pinero's play, *The Princess and the Butterfly*.

For such a tribute, Raven-Hill, a fine artist and a most discerning art-editor, must get the credit. He attracted work from some of the best French draughtsmen of the day – Caran d'Ache, Job, Gerbault and Willette – and he recruited Phil May and Max Beerbohm. When Sime joined the magazine in 1895, the regular artists included Lewis Baumer,

'Ye Shades', after-life cartoon for *Pick-Me-Up*, 1895

Will Owen, Dudley Hardy, Maurice Greiffenhagen, Edgar Wilson, J. W. T. Manuel, Oscar Eckhardt and G. D. Armour. It was excellent company for Sime to keep.

Raven-Hill started another magazine in 1895, the *Unicorn*, and, as often happened at that time, it ran for only three issues. Sime contributed to it a fine satirical fantasy, 'The Pursuit of Pleasure', in which he appeared to relish the dark fate in store for all sybarites.

The Minster, New Series, starting in January 1896, with the enlivening team of Raven-Hill, Manuel and Sime, reinforced by Gordon Craig, Fred Pegram and Byam Shaw, lasted for three issues as well. Sime's full-page cartoon in the February number showed a layabout addressing a queue of unemployed and was captioned 'Ello Mates – Any danger of a job?' It was his first pictorial comment on his own times and it was seldom to be repeated. In March he had some porcine illustrations to a story called *The Bacon of the Future*.

They were delightfully drawn; Sime clearly had an affection for the pig and an awareness of its comic potential. Many of his own fantastic creatures have a pig-like foundation.

In 1896 Sime was a prolific contributor to *Pick-Me-Up*. On 4 April there appeared the first of the theatrical caricatures he was to draw for the regular feature, 'Through the Opera Glass', written by Arnold Golsworthy under the pseudonym 'Jingle'. The two men soon became friends and on 13 June Golsworthy called him, for the first time, 'the man Sime' – a soubriquet that stuck.

From then on Golsworthy had a lot of affectionate fun at Sime's expense. One evening they had to sit in the pit:

I didn't mind so much for myself but I thought of the man Sime, this delicately nurtured, elegant creature; and I hardly knew how I would be able to break to him the news that he, the chosen person of modern art, the favourite of fortune, would have to shuffle into the pit with me as best he might . . .

The jocular references became ever more complimentary.

Once inside the box, however, the usual unseemly wrangle followed as to whether I or the man Sime should occupy the corner chair that commanded the best view of the stage. I shall have to talk rather straight to this person soon . . .
Ever since the daily papers came out with a lot of guff about

'Dan Leno, comedian', etching

his last painting there has been no suppressing the man at all. To hear him talk you'd think he was quite as good as I am.

There are abusive allusions to Sime's liking for a drink, to his poor shooting ability and to his *outré* appearance, especially his taste in neckties. On Sime's part there are three splendid drawings of himself and 'Jingle' in which he goes some way towards levelling the score with his partner.

Sime caricatured all the great names of the music hall and theatre and for two of them he seems to have had a particular affection – Dan Leno and Sarah Bernhardt.

He devoted a good deal of care to these theatrical drawings, as he told E. S. Valentine in an interview published in the *Strand Magazine*, October 1908:

It took me some time to study an actor's mannerisms so as to give a characteristic picture of him. I usually visited a piece two or three times before making my finished sketch. At the first visit I would study his face from the stalls; at the second visit I might consider him from a dark corner of the pit, noting his peculiarities of gesture and attitude.

There are many sketch-books at Worplesdon filled with studies for the finished drawings.

EN ROUTE.

Arnold Golsworthy and Sidney Sime, caricature, 1897

The care taken by Sime was appreciated by David Low, the cartoonist, writing in 1947:

The most notable [of the theatrical caricaturists of the Nineties] was S. H. Sime, a beautifully imaginative artist, with a mordant fancy which sometimes overlaid his observation of character, but whose studies of people nevertheless are full of true and well-balanced caricature. No mere vulgar sprawling irresponsibility about him, but a patient individual appraisement in his own terms.

Sime contributed twenty-three full-page political cartoons to *Pick-Me-Up*, starting on 26 August 1896 and ending on 13 February 1897. Sime was often referred to as a deep thinker but these cartoons provide no indication that he thought much about politics; in the main they do no more than reflect the

'By the banks of the Styx – a facer', after-life cartoon for *Pick-Me-Up*, 1896

'Sarah Bernhardt as Hamlet', illustration for the *Butterfly*, 1899

popular attitudes and prejudices of the day. It was as well that they were curtailed otherwise Sime's talents might have been misused, as E. H. Shepard's were to be in a later generation.

During 1896 Sime contributed five more 'Shades' pictures to *Pick-Me-Up*, two of which reveal him at the top of his form. 'By the banks of the Styx – a facer' is full of pointed and humorous observation, and is the first drawing in which his remarkable skill in conveying textures can be seen. 'I say, I only know "All in a row" and "Beer, glorious beer"' has two of the best heads that he ever drew.

It must have been on the strength of his fantasy drawings that Sime was invited to contribute to the *Idler*, his work making its first appearance there in February 1896. The *Idler* had been founded in 1892 by Jerome K. Jerome for 'people of literary tastes and artistic sympathies' (a different class from the readers of *Pick-Me-Up*).

To begin with, it was the 'literary tastes' not the 'artistic sympathies' which were gratified and even after he had promised reform, when he became editor in 1895, Jerome never achieved his high ambition 'to make every illustration a picture worth looking at'.

This is not surprising, considering the lamentable standard of artwork in *Today*, a magazine he had edited for several years.

But he did improve matters during 1896 with the introduction of Sime in February, Pegram in March and Manuel in November. Sime found his length with his second drawing, a 'Shades' picture called 'More Birds of a Feather' and his last contribution that year, 'Waiting for the Boatman', was a 'fizzer'.

Like many other illustrators of the day, Sime often composed on a large scale. The original drawings for these two pictures measure 50 × 35 cms and were reduced to 16.5 × 11.5 cms in reproduction. They are on Bristol board and had been preceded by sketches on paper. The media Sime used in these drawings included wash, charcoal, ink and lampblack with Chinese white or grey body-colour for the highlights – a variety that must have posed many problems for the printers in those relatively early days of half-tone and that occasionally defeated them. Sime worked his media with brushes, pens, knives and sponges; it was his constant aim to make his pictures more mysterious and for this purpose he used means that were beyond the scope of most illustrators. His approach was that of a painter, concerned with textures and tones and lighting.

* * *

In December 1897 there appeared in the *Windsor Magazine* the first estimate of Sime's ranking in the world of illustrators, which shows how far he had travelled since his first appearance in *Pick-Me-Up* just two years before. The writer talks about 'an oligarchy, so to speak of extremely clever artists, a select few whose work differing in style and subject, is alike in the exhibition of the finest artistic qualities and the full appreciation of the black and white medium'. The five who were singled out (none of them contributors to the *Windsor Magazine*) were Raven-Hill, Greiffenhagen, E. Wilson, Armour and Sime.

The year 1897 was one of progress for Sime. In *Pick-Me-Up* he continued to provide insights into the after-life and sketch theatrical celebrities. In the *Idler* he explored a new vein in a series of purely fantastic drawings called 'From an Ultimate Dim Thule', wherein much artistry was captioned with much laboured nonsense. And in that year he contributed to *Eureka*, of which he became editor.

Eureka, in its opening number, had printed one of those declarations to which editors were prone:

Neither in its letterpress, nor in its illustrations, which will be numerous and of high quality, will anything be found offensive to good taste, or to that sense of propriety, which decent Britons demand of those whom they introduce into the drawing rooms of their private houses.

Sime soon put a stop to that. 'The Felon Flower', a poem he chose to illustrate in the September issue with a full-page drawing, was a real spine-chiller:

'I say, I only know "All in a row" and "Beer, glorious beer"', after-life cartoon for *Pick-Me-Up*, 1896

'More Birds of a Feather', after-life cartoon for the *Idler*, 1896

'Waiting for the Boatman', after-life cartoon for the *Idler*, 1896

She eyes the flesh not yet begun to rot
And screams a hollow laugh that evil bodes
For lo! 'twill simmer bravely in the pot
When mixed with precious venom squeezed from toads.

It appears that Sime edited *Eureka* from the autumn of 1897 until February 1898 (when the last of his drawings appears) and that his devotion to duty was sporadic. In September we hear, 'We have mislaid our Editor' and in November, 'the Editor has come back. We understood that he had gone to Brighton for the benefit of his health, and were subsequently much pained to receive a hurried note from Paris, saying that he was having a really good time, and urging us to work very hard indeed, since there was a dignity in labour which surpassed the majesty of Kings.'

'Jingle' again? It would tie up with Lawrence's comment in the *Idler*, January 1898: 'of late Messers Sime and Golsworthy have been still further associated in the conduct of a threepenny magazine, entitled *Eureka* . . . it seems that Mr Sime edits it and Mr Golsworthy "patronises it".' Sime's editorship may have been intermittent but he introduced a number of talented artists such as Raven-Hill and Manuel.

Sime did no more theatrical caricatures for *Pick-Me-Up* after 12 March. He had finished with 'Ye Shades' for the time being also: 'it was understood that the proprietors of the paper were of the opinion that the drawings were calculated to wound the religious susceptibilities of the public', said the critic of the *Windsor Magazine*, though he disagreed himself and called in 'a most important dignitary of the church' to back him up. It was the *Ludgate Magazine*, New Series, which had the best of his work – illustrations in a playful diabolical style.

* * *

In 1898, Sime's uncle, William Sime, died. Unlike his brother, William Sime had been prosperous, having worked as a solicitor in Edinburgh. He bequeathed his Edinburgh house, its contents and £3,000 to a friend. The rest, 'the residue of my whole means and estate', he left to 'my nephew Sidney Herbert Sime artist presently in London'. Sime was now worth over £14,000, and could afford to move to the comfort of his uncle's second residence, Daldrishaig, Aberfoyle, Perthshire.

The hard start in life; the move to the great city; a hard-won professional success; now a legacy: it sounds like the plot of a romantic story. The next event followed the pattern. Thorpe tells the tale: 'One day when he was studying the watercolours at South Kensington, a chance reflection of a face in the glass of a dark picture aroused his interest. A request to borrow an unnecessary tube of lamp-black led to an introduction and later, in 1898, to his marriage in Edinburgh to Mary Susan Pickett.'

Mary was an artist too. Her work appeared in *Pick-Me-Up* and, before their marriage, Sime had

Portrait in oils of Mary Susan Pickett by Sidney Sime

introduced her to *Eureka*, but she was mainly a painter of miniatures. She had had work accepted by the Royal Academy. In the year of their wedding, she exhibited a painting of 'Little Nell in the Old Church', a subject taken from *The Old Curiosity Shop*.

Now a married man of property, Sime settled in Scotland with his wife and took the opportunity to develop as a painter. The Worplesdon collection contains a number of Scottish landscapes, some of which were seen at a Langham *conversazione* in 1898. Small in scale and very distinctive in quality, they are halfway to being, in Gerard Manley Hopkins's phrase, 'inscapes', landscapes with a visible sense of a moving force beyond the actual hills, trees or sky.

Around this time, Sime used a substantial part of his new fortune to buy the *Idler*, installing himself as co-editor in May 1899.

There was an immediate change of cover-design, intended to herald a new approach. The previous 'Idler' had been a benevolent old gentleman smoking a clay pipe; Sime's 'Idler' was a decadent-looking dandy with a cane. The colours of black, red and cream gave place to grey and violet. There were new contributors on the literary side and new artists, amongst whom Philip Connard stands out with some notably epicene drawings. But the promise of the cover-change was not really fulfilled, apart from

Sime's own contributions. He did not seem to have Raven-Hill's ability to attract artists as good as himself and he needed to do this because the *Idler*, in its class, was expensive. Sime would have been well advised to heed the warning expressed by the *Oxford Chronicle*, which, having been complimentary about the changes, then observed: 'We may still feel the editors are courting unpopularity by keeping the *Idler* at 1/– when it has so many formidable rivals at 6d'. The *Strand*, the *Windsor*, *Pearson's* and the *English Illustrated Magazine* all sold for 6d. Only the *Pall Mall Magazine* cost 1/-, even 1/6d at times, but it was a periodical of much greater substance.

* * *

The *Pall Mall Magazine*, started in 1893 and edited by Lord Frederic Hamilton, can be singled out as the only monthly magazine to ensure that both the literary and the artistic contributions remained on a consistently high level. Sime arrived in January 1899 and the volume in which his first contributions appeared is admirable. Edmund J. Sullivan, in a series of illustrations to a piece of science-fiction by H. G. Wells, demonstrated skills that caused a writer fourteen years later in the *Art Chronicle* to say: 'his work [Sullivan] and Aubrey Beardsley's will best represent the movements of the past and present generation to the future historians of the illustration of books'. There were fine drawings too from Patten Wilson, Claude Shepperson, Maurice Greiffenhagen, Herbert Cole, A. S. Hartrick, Lewis Baumer, Nico Jungman, G. D. Armour, Herbert Railton, G. R. Halkett and Granville Fell. Some of these were wash drawings, and they were well reproduced for the *Pall Mall* printed half-tones far better than most of its contemporaries.

In 1899 Sime also contributed spirited little vignettes to a regular feature in the *Pall Mall* called 'From a London Attic'. By far his most important drawings, however, because they clearly foreshadow the work he was to do with Dunsany, were the illustrations he drew for a fantasy by Laurence Housman in the March issue. It was called 'The Mountains of the Moon' and the first paragraph is quoted to give an idea of its Gothic flavour:

Gundre sat by his father's bed, waiting till the old man should die. All round him lay the weapons of the chase, each one ready for use, and the door stood wide, giving a glimpse of the moonlit forest swaying its black shadows in the wind. High overhead the great rock which is known as the Giant's Larder rose heavy against the night; solid and square it stood, and at its base the forest shook and moaned.

It was the first time that Sime had been given a story presenting a real challenge. The illustrations reek of dread and ancient mystery; none more so than the one captioned '"Pass forth, brother," said the Dark Huntsman, "who knowest the secrets of the dead."'

* * *

The *Butterfly*, New Series, starting in March 1899, was an attempt by the publisher, Grant Richards, to revive the style but avoid the fate of a previous publication of the same name edited by Arnold Golsworthy and Raven-Hill which had fluttered prettily between May 1893 and February 1894. James Thorpe, in *English Illustration: The Nineties*, wrote (referring to both series):

No magazine, in England at any rate, has contained in a short life of twenty-two months such a wonderful collection of black-and-white work. From this point of view it is undoubtedly the most artistic periodical we have ever had, fully representative of the best work of the nineties and its failure is a reflection on the deplorable lack of intelligence and appreciation in this country.

The artists of the original *Butterfly* loomed large in the new venture. Raven-Hill, Greiffenhagen and E. Wilson provided drawings, cartoons and decorations. They were joined by Manuel, Beerbohm and Sime.

In the *Butterfly* the full range of Sime's artistic talents is revealed. He reverted to his preoccupation with the next world in such drawings as 'Over There' and 'A Practised Hand', and did so with a new sophistication. A drawing called 'The Incubus' (later coloured and reproduced in the *Magazine of Art*) reminds one of Henry Fuseli's 'The Nightmare'. Other fine drawings were 'Incense', commended for its 'sheer beauty' by Richard Le Gallienne, 'The Banshee' and 'Sarah Bernhardt as Hamlet'.

A particularly interesting picture was 'On Desperate Seas', published in April; not only was it beautiful and mysterious but it stimulated the editor, Edgar Wilson, to compete. His own *Making for Plymouth* appeared in August.

The second volume of the *Butterfly*, New Series, is nowhere near as good as the first. 'Sea Song' by Sime is an agreeably weird drawing but in general his contributions, mostly wash drawings, are not well reproduced. Despite this, they still had admirers. The *Butterfly*, when it died in February 1900, did so not so much because of 'the deplorable lack of intelligence and appreciation in this country', but because the half-tones were below standard and because the literary content had never been distinguished.

* * *

Sime's year of greatest achievement in the magazines and the high point of his career was unquestionably 1899. Haldane Macfall, a critic of some repute who was to write many books on art, noticed Sime's work in the September issue of *St Paul's*. 'Though Beardsley', wrote Macfall, 'must remain for all time an exquisite master of line and head of the grotesque school, Sime has certain qualities in which, on the other hand, Beardsley never approached him. There is behind all Sime's work an extraordinary sense of one who has felt the immensity of life.' And Macfall concluded his article with a forecast which many would have echoed at the time: 'it requires no great prophet to foretell that Sime will be one of our greatest black-and-white artists. . .'

Illustration by Sidney Sime for 'The Mountains of the Moon', fantasy by Laurence Housman, *Pall Mall Magazine*, 1899

Yet in 1900 he started to fade. Though he supplied the *Idler* with some fine pictures – of which 'In Faery Lands Forlorn', 'At Elsinore' and 'Spring Heeled Jack' were outstanding – many of its readers must have experienced a strong sense of *déjà vu*. Every one of Sime's nine illustrations appearing in the November and December issues had been printed in the *Butterfly* the year before.

We do not know what price Sime paid for the *Idler* but, according to Thorpe, there had been 'an accumulation of bad debts, skilfully concealed from him at the time of purchase' and in 1901 'he sold the goodwill, such as it was, for £5'. Certainly he lost a good deal of money over the transaction and his policy as editor of reprinting his own work so soon after publication cannot have helped his reputation. However he did get some fun out of it. He published

'In Faery Lands Forlorn', illustration for the *Idler*, 1900

'Midnight Oil', illustration for the *Idler*, 1899

some decorative head and tail pieces by his wife and a full-page drawing of hers, 'Shagpat', which reminds one of their shared passion for George Meredith. He also published some work by his friend Duncan Tovey, an accomplished musician and song-writer and a fellow member of the Yorick Club.

After the *Idler* débâcle he seemed to lose enthusiasm for magazine work. There were a few more contributions to the *Pall Mall Magazine*, the best being 'The End of All Knowledge' and a series of twelve illustrated nursery rhymes which appeared between 1901 and 1905. They were unconventional: to ask Sime to illustrate a nursery rhyme was like asking Beardsley to design a Christmas card. In 1902 Sime had two drawings printed in *Punch*: the 'Imperturbable Boatman' is well drawn and a good deal funnier than most *Punch* jokes of the period. For the *Strand Magazine* he did some mildly comic drawings from time to time and five illustrations to an article in the December 1905 issue called 'Haschisch Hallucinations': it was a subject which sparked off his imagination and the vivid drawings cry out for reproduction on a larger scale. That, apart from his work for the illustrated weeklies which is discussed below, completes his post-1900 output for the magazines. His dislike of them increased over the years as can be seen in a letter he wrote to his friend, the composer Josef Holbrooke, on 18 August 1910. Sime urged him to avoid 'the worst possible form of publication – magazines! Those God-forsaken sponge-cakes of the surburban soul.'

There were two important articles on Sime's work after 1900. The *Magazine of Art* had been no friend to Sime the painter when he exhibited at the Royal Society of British Artists in the late Nineties, but in 1904 it published a sympathetic appreciation of his graphic work by Frank Emanuel, a fellow artist. The writer made comparisons between Sime's work and that of Beardsley, Blake and Goya, called attention to the beauty in several of Sime's drawings for the *Idler* and 'the warmheartedness underlying the artist's devilry', and ended with this tribute:

Mr Sime is as eloquent and vivacious in his speech as with his pencil, and, modest though he be, he is markedly a man of great individuality and deep thought. A vast forehead dominates a face indicative of strength, while a certain appearance of grimness is frequently dispelled by a humorous twinkle of the eye and the most genial of smiles. In short, he looks every inch the author of his drawings, in equal part an irresistible humorist, an original thinker and a truly inventive artist.

In the *Strand*, October 1908, there is an account of an interview between Sime and E. S. Valentine in which Sime was more than usually forthcoming about his attitude to art. 'What I do', he said, 'I don't do consciously. I have a natural inherent bent towards mystery, and things must appear to be touched with what I may call the "bogey wand" or – well, I simply don't see them! . . . I'm afraid the general public wants what is obvious and instantly understood . . . If an artist's work can't be understood at once people think he is posing. Well, perhaps he is posing. I'm not.'

* * *

It is appropriate to consider separately Sime's illustrations for the weeklies, the *Illustrated London News, Sketch, Tatler* and *Graphic*, in which almost all of his work appeared after the turn of the century, because they offered him quite different opportunities. The object of these magazines was to record the passing scene of public affairs, society, sport and drama and the principal means used was photography. A few artists such as Caton Woodville and Fortunino Matania were employed as reporters but in the main artists were required to be noticeable, to provide arresting contrasts, to entertain – and they were given the space to do so. All these magazines were large, folio size, and printed on good quality art paper; the standard of reproduction was superior to anything Sime had experienced elsewhere and the increased scale usually suited him.

Sime's appearances were infrequent and he owed them to the support of Bruce Ingram, editor of the *Illustrated London News* and owner at some time of a financial interest in all the other illustrated weeklies in which Sime's work appeared. Bruce Ingram, as Sime said with justified conviction in a letter to Josef Holbrooke, is 'nuts on my drawings'.

The *Illustrated London News* was proud of its connection with Sime and certainly he had no stouter champion. Yet, strangely enough, it printed little of his work. In November 1892 there appeared his drawing, 'Overtime', a sick-bed scene, which harked back to the morbid sentimentality of a previous generation. There was nothing else until December 1909 when two small photographs of Sime's stage-designs for Maurice Maeterlinck's play *The Blue Bird* were published. In October the following year there were three photographs of the Adelsberg Grotto, a stalactite cavern, under the heading 'Nature in Rivalry with Sime'. In 1912 and 1914 there were photographs of Sime's designs for *The Children of Don* and *Dylan*, operas by Lord Howard and Holbrooke. It was not until the 1920 Christmas number that the first fantasy picture – 'The God of the Yule month: Thor shut out from Valhalla' – appeared.

In this picture Sime surpasses himself. All that he sensed in pagan romance, all the mystery and magic of the old gods, is there. It is a volcanic composition which gives meaning to Macfall's phrase that in Sime's work we hear 'the thunder of immensity'.

In April 1922 the *Illustrated London News* reproduced Sime's frontispiece for Dunsany's *Chronicles of Rodriguez* and called him 'an artist of acknowledged genius whose work is familiar to our readers' and in November of the same year it published an article on his work, 'The Genius of Sidney H. Sime', by Major Haldane Macfall, accompanied by one of his best pictures, 'The Forest of Shadow Valley'.

The magazine was disposed to take credit for its actions:

'Shagpat, the Son of Shimpoor', drawing by Mary Susan Pickett for the *Idler*, 1900

Imperturbable Boatman: "Haud up yer rod, man! Ye have'm! Ye have'm!" Cartoon for *Punch*, 1902

'The Flight of the Gods to Valhalla', illustration for the
Illustrated London News, 1920

Although it may be true that the genius of Sime has been
overlooked by the academic world of art, as Mr. Haldane
Macfall suggests in the enthusiastic eulogy of his friend
that we print on the opposite page, this paper at least can
claim to have done its part towards establishing his fame.

Macfall's eulogy was enthusiastic to the point of
absurdity:

Sime ranges free and unfettered and wide – his flight is
limitless. He leaps into the immensities and is reckless of the
eternities. Indeed more than once he has been indiscreet
enough to be familiar with the vastnesses . . .

Hyperbole like this could only do harm to an artist,
especially when there had been few chances of seeing
his work.

In the 1922 Christmas number, alongside illustrations by Kay Nielsen, Edmund Dulac, Georges
Barbier and E. J. Detmold, there appeared two full-
page drawings by Sime, 'Indra quenching the flames
of Agni' and 'Echidna Dire, Mother of Monsters',
under the heading 'The Symbolism of Sime'.

In June 1924 came two of Sime's finest fantasies,
'Hunting the Unicorn' and 'The Ship comes Home'.
The first was the frontispiece to Dunsany's *The King of
Elfland's Daughter*. The second, an Apocalyptic scene,
contains most of the elements that made up Sime's
imaginary world – seas, cliffs, lighthouse, stars, moon,
comets, thunderbolts and a black sky, all lit dramati-
cally and given a strange intensity of feeling.

The 1925 Christmas number had a picture entitled
'A Cornish Christmas Litany'. It was described as
'this characteristic drawing of S. H. Sime who is so
well known as a master of fantasy'. It must have been
about this drawing that James Thorpe tells the
following story:

He once gave a young lady a drawing of a crowd of men in
panic trying to force their way through the closed door of a
cottage. They are pursued by all sorts of writhing malignant
forms. She was fascinatedly grateful. 'Ah!' said Sime 'you
don't know the real point of it. It's far worse when they get
inside.'

There was little more of Sime in the *Illustrated
London News*. The 1926 Christmas number had 'The
Castle of our Dreams: Chateaurien'. The Christmas
numbers for 1931 and 1932 had reproductions in
colour of two rather insipid paintings which had been
shown in Sime's 1927 exhibition – 'Floating Island'
and 'Off the coast of Albania'.

Sime's contributions to the *Illustrated London News*
have been dealt with at some length, partly because
they have not previously been recorded and partly
because in the 1920s they included some remarkable
work. The fact that the paper had virtually ignored
him before this time may have reminded Sime of Dr
Johnson's celebrated remonstrance to Lord Chester-
field: 'Is not a patron, my lord, one who looks with
unconcern on a man struggling for life in the water,
and, when he has reached ground, encumbers him
with help?'

* * *

The *Sketch* was an offshoot of the *Illustrated London
News* and pioneer of the 'New Illustrated Journal-
ism', based on the use of photography and the
extension of subject matter. It was a lively magazine,
to which Sime's work was far more suited than to the
Illustrated London News, and it was to carry far more of
it.

Sime's first appearance in the *Sketch* came in May
1897 with 'Dreams, Idle Dreams'. It is one of his most
celebrated drawings and Lord Dunsany was clearly
thinking of it when he wrote in the *Fortnightly Review*:

Houses of his in cliffs, and even in trees, fill the world with a
new wonder for us, but one which we should not be quite
able to enjoy, finding it too far outside our experience, were
it not for a stovepipe coming out of the cliff or the tree, a
stovepipe so common in its design that not one of us can
complain this is too far-fetched.

Another Sime classic, 'The Gate of Heaven',
appeared in the *Sketch* Christmas Supplement,
December 1903. A brilliant satire on riches, it stays in
the mind like the best of Hilaire Belloc's epigrams.

The next year Sime contributed a series of three
'Tragi-Comedies' to the *Sketch*, powerfully drawn
fantasies which comment on the sad fate of the
entertainer and which, in their overt symbolism, are
different from the bulk of his work.

Between 18 January and 22 March 1905 the *Sketch*
published a series of twelve drawings called 'The

"I dreamed that I was the Woman of Char, and that it was my task to scrub the endless and gigantic stairs which are neither here nor there. I had no water, but my tears fell in great abundance, and there was an occasional shower: so I worked frantically, and the lather grew and grew and grew. But despair overcame me when I realised the hideous mockery of the situation – *the stairs were made of soap*!" 'The Dream of the Woman of Char', illustration for the *Sketch*, 1905.

Sime Zoology: Beasts that might have been'. (Ten of these, touched up a little and in one case renamed, were joined by five others and published in 1923 as 'Bogey Beasts', a book of pictures and verses by Sime with music by Josef Holbrooke.) Sime's creatures are a rather boneless lot with a tendency to shyness and a propensity for nocturnal wandering – if one were to be confronted with them, they would surely be the first to run away. Artistically the most interesting thing about many of these pictures is the foreground. Those in 'The Long Eared Bloog', 'The Two Tailed Sogg' and 'The Wily Grasser' are full of intricate detail, giving the pictures a richly textured effect.

There were other good full-page drawings by Sime in the *Sketch* of 1905 and 1906; best of all is 'The Dream of the Woman of Char', a delicious fantasy with (for once) an apt and amusing caption.

In 1910 came a series which suggested that the editor's imagination was being pushed beyond its natural limits. It was called 'The Aurae of the Drama' and was introduced with these words: 'Each play has its aura, a subtle something that rises from it and, working on the brain, creates impressions. Realising this, we have asked Mr. Sime to visit a number of the theatres and to do for us a series of drawings, not of the plays seen but of the impressions made upon his mind by those plays.' What an assignment! It is hard to say how successful Sime was in conveying the 'aurae'

(supposing the feat to be possible) as most of the plays are now forgotten.

Sime's last contribution to the *Sketch* was the magnificent series of pictures for which Dunsany wrote stories, later published under the title of *The Book of Wonder*, and his illustrations for Dunsany's *Tales of Wonder*, which are described below.

* * *

The *Tatler* came from the same stable as the *Sphere* and was at first owned by the printers and publishers Eyre and Spottiswoode. It was started in July 1901 by Clement Shorter and intended as a rival to the *Sketch*. Its opening editorial made no startling claims:

We are going to deal with society and the drama even more brightly and genially than they have been dealt with elsewhere. We are going to take things as we find them, to make the most and the best of them, and to give the public as many illustrations of them as can be crowded into our space.

The opening numbers 'were pronounced to be dull' according to Shorter. That was to overlook Sime's contribution.

The *Tatler* lost no time in securing Sime's services. In August 1901 there appeared 'Drawing to Unknown Tales', one of his most elaborate fantasies, a masterpiece of horrifying humour. In August of the

'The Ship comes Home', illustration for the *Illustrated London News*, 1924

following year came 'Tchaikowsky's Sugar-Plum Fairy Dance' described correctly in the caption as 'This curious drawing', and a vigorous rendering of 'The Spanish Dancer Tortajada at the Alhambra'. In August 1903, surprisingly enough, Sime supplied a political cartoon. It was far more impressive than anything of this sort he had done for *Pick-Me-Up*, with excellent characterization of Joseph Chamberlain and Lloyd George. In January 1905 there was 'A Storyette', a delicate fantasy with overtones of dread in the caption. Sime's final contribution to the *Tatler* was in 1906, a weak invention by his standards.

Admirers of Sime's theatrical caricatures had a last chance to see his work in the *Tatler* between June 1902 and May 1904. Once more he was teamed with Arnold Golsworthy, and it was a fruitful partnership. They visited the music halls at fortnightly or three-weekly intervals: the Oxford, the Tivoli, the Alhambra, the Empire and the Palace. The badinage was much as before:

When a manager catches my eye first he usually steps towards us with the right hand of fellowship ready for use; but if his glance falls on the man Sime's hat first he pulls up short and then goes back to count the spoons or something of that sort.

Sime's drawing did not always have the sparkle of his *Pick-Me-Up* days; on the other hand, the occasional catastrophe of that time was absent too, perhaps because he had more time for the job as well as greater maturity. Towards the end of this stint he seemed to tire. At one point Golsworthy teased: 'but these artists exaggerate so much you can never rely on them. Look at the man's drawings this week for instance; I wonder they keep him on, I do really.' Probably Sime had had enough by then of cake-walks, skirt dances and coloured coons.

* * *

The *Graphic* was the last of the news-magazines to publish Sime's work. In November 1922 there appeared in it a double-page article with ten illustrations headed 'Sime, the Prophet in Line'. It was by the popular journalist Hannen Swaffer, and was No. 5 in a series 'People I Know'. Swaffer ended his piece with a prophecy:

Yes, for years, Sime with his pencil laughed at the bogies of mid-Victorian days. His humour was a mixture of savagery and insight. And, now that he has destroyed much that needed removal, he is living in a small village doing work which, one day, will astonish all the thinking world.

In its Christmas number, the *Graphic* published *The Travel Tales of Mr. Joseph Jorkens* by Lord Dunsany, with five watercolour illustrations by Sime. The colouring is gentle and pleasant and the drawings have a mischievous charm which suits the text.

* * *

Sime in no way conformed to the normal pattern of a magazine illustrator. Each week Phil May, George Belcher, H. M. Bateman and Heath Robinson would provide good drawings, more or less funny according to inspiration, exploiting a particular theme. Their consistency could be depended upon, as could the consistency of story illustrators like Hugh Thomson, Edmund Sullivan, Maurice Greiffenhagen and the Brocks. For a brief moment it looked as if Sime had found a theme as rich as Heath Robinson's 'Inventions' or the 'Outrages' of Bateman. But 'Ye Shades' retired and thereafter Sime, apart from his theatrical caricatures, created pictures for reproduction rather than illustrations of a theme or text. The subjects of those pictures varied hugely: the only constant was the mystery.

The magazine editors reproduced much of Sime's work badly; they tended to type-cast him; they paid him badly and imposed deadlines. For the man who told Hannen Swaffer, 'Art does not lie in performance: it is a mental condition' the conditions must have been irksome. Yet we can be grateful to those editors for they disseminated much of Sime's best work, and we are especially indebted to Bruce Ingram for reproducing Sime's work on a fitting scale.

Painter and Clubman

Although Sime earned his living as an illustrator, he still cherished ambitions of becoming a painter. In

1896 he became a member of the Royal Society of British Artists, together with two friends from the magazine world, Oscar Eckhardt and J. W. T. Manuel.

The Society was founded in 1823, fifty-five years after the establishment of the Royal Academy. Throughout the Victorian period it had given large exhibitions which provided a market place in which artists could sell their wares; there were few commercial galleries even at the end of the century. 'Suffolk Street', as it became known from the site of the gallery, did not have the same prestige as the Royal Academy. After a brief period during which James Whistler was president, introducing Aestheticism and Good Taste, and throwing out the traditional paintings, the then Royal Society tended to be a dull place. Whistler left with the famous taunt, 'The artists have come out, the British remain.'

Sime, who had never before shown at Suffolk Street, was not only a member but also a council member for the Winter Exhibition of 1896. He exhibited two portraits which were not for sale and so had prestige and were non-competitive. The reviewer for the *Magazine of Art*, whose articles were continually and deliberately unsympathetic to this 'group of three', gave a mention to 'Mr. Sime's flat portrait of a gentleman'.

In the Winter Exhibition of 1897 Sime had, in addition to a portrait, two pictures which were for sale, 'The Peacock Fan' and 'The Lonely Road'. The next year Sime and his two friends made a concerted attack on the Summer Exhibition. A portrait by Sime was hung in the prime spot in the Central Gallery and the vestibule, the prestigious separate section, was completely taken over by Sime, Eckhardt and Manuel. These three, with their raciness of style and in their subject matter, which ranged from blunt observation of 'low' life to the provocatively strange, must have stood out from the rest like brown boots at a funeral.

The amount of space that the *Magazine of Art* devotes to the group's work at this exhibition indicates the impact that they made. For reasons best known to himself, the reviewer credits the work of all three in the vestibule to Manuel. 'The position usually occupied by Mr. Cayley Robinson's work is this year given up to Mr. S. H. Sime's strikingly clever "portrait" of a lady, which proves that he can attract attention pleasantly, as well as by the *outré* productions with which his name has hitherto been associated. . . . The vestibule is given up entirely to a series of sketches of London Streets and other scenes by Mr. Manuel – some grotesque, some a little vulgar, but all clever.'

The next year, Manuel died, and Sime and Eckhardt seemed to lose interest in Suffolk Street. In 1899 Sime left the council and he disappeared from the list of members in 1903. The picture he exhibited at the Winter Exhibition of 1900, however, evoked this comment from *The Artist*: 'A little *Model with Accessories* by S. H. Sime is, perhaps, the most painter-like picture of the whole exhibition. Painted with a touch which reminds one of Manet at his best, and least brutal, it reveals an admirable knowledge of tone-values.'

* * *

Sime very probably joined the Langham Sketching Club before he became a member of the R.B.A. It provided a studio to work in several evenings a week and a model to work from. This was its prime *raison d'être* and we can see that Sime took advantage of these facilities: in a folder at Worplesdon there is a seductive little etching of a nude posing on 'the throne', inscribed 'Langham, April 99'. The Langham also provided a reference library and a wardrobe of historical costumes, both invaluable for an illustrator. In 1904 the *Studio* published an article about it:

Tucked snugly beneath the wing of All Souls, away from the noise and hurry of London, one comes upon the oldest of all the Sketching Clubs in the world – the Langham. Nothing could be more simple and unassuming than are its rooms, and the narrow cul-de-sac leading up to them, but many famous men have come and gone within its membership for three quarters of a century, and the imprint of its influence must always be felt on English art.

The Langham Artists' Society was founded in 1830. This was limited in number, but its dependent Sketching Club had a wider membership and was not difficult to join.

In many respects the club was similar to a medieval guild of craftsmen. The members were professionals; there was training for the young, and regular convivial evenings with beer, simple food and entertainment provided by the members themselves. The membership was always wide and had included artists like Pinwell, Keene and Walker, associated with the great period of illustration in the Sixties. A contemporary of Sime, who later went over to the 'London', a splinter group of the Langham, was Dudley Hardy, whose poster for the *Idler*, entitled 'The Yellow Girl', started the poster craze, and gave another adjective to the Nineties. It may well have been here that Sime's friendship with the painter Walter Bayes and also with W. G. Johnson began. The latter was to be a close friend, collaborator in theatrical ventures, near-neighbour, and perpetual fall-guy for Sime's gags.

Among the most important events in the Langham calendar were the *conversazioni*, of which there were three a year. Members gave informal shows of their work, providing entertainment and hospitality for their guests. It was at one of these gatherings that two of Sime's greatest admirers, Arthur Lawrence and James Thorpe, met him for the first time. Sime exhibited his work and Lawrence, reviewing an 1898 *conversazione* for *Today*, wrote, 'Mr Sime, who has only just returned from the ambrosial ravines of Aberfoyle, contributes several 'scapes as the outcome of his perambulations near his country estate.'

Etching inscribed 'Langham, April 99'

Thorpe recollects:

My earliest memory of Sime, forty years ago, at the Langham Sketch Club *conversazioni*, is of a slim figure, slightly above average height, with a rather large head, crowned with a thick mop of black hair. His family called him 'Tad' – short for tadpole. His expression was very striking and would have been described by the lady novelists of the period as sardonic, with a smile always playing around his mouth. He had a thin black beard which grew in two points. Someone has said that he only wanted two short horns to resemble those little figures of devils which he drew so often and so convincingly. He was quiet and reserved in temperament because of his wisdom, but he had a quick and biting gift of repartee, more conclusive than cruel. He preferred a few friends, choice kindred spirits, to a crowd.

* * *

Sime also had another haunt – the Yorick Club, just off the Strand. The Yorick did not attract big names, but the members – men of the theatre or connected with the arts, journalists, adventurers – were all men with stories to tell. The club is described by Pett Ridge in his memoirs, *A Story Teller: Forty Years in London*, published in 1923.

'The subscription was two guineas a year, and the entrance fee two guineas. It had cosy rooms on a second floor in Beaufort Buildings, a cul-de-sac, and of an evening we could see the Savoy players go in at their stage door. The club opened at noon and shut at two o'clock in the morning; it had a proprietor who consented to allow himself to be called House Manager, and he ran the club with remarkable skill. The club remained at Beaufort Buildings for nine years; when the Strand alterations began, it moved to Bedford Street on the left hand of an entrance to St Paul's, Covent Garden . . .

At Bedford Street the rooms were larger and more convenient; our landlord was a publisher [J. M. Dent] who ever talked darkly of turning us out. We had a Master of Revels in George Parlby, a Director of Music in Duncan Tovey; Sime was Director of Art, and I was Librarian. The annual dinners at Monico's showed us at our best and smartest. Max Beerbohm spoke there more than once. . . . No one was permitted to brag unduly, and if you could play or sing you had, when the occasion happened, to play or sing.

Sime, the Director of Art, not only provided drawings for menu-cards, but also did caricatures of the members, and his appearances in the club with a parcel under his arm gave rise to a certain uneasiness in members who were not already enframed on the wall. But many were well pleased and the caricatures were hung up in the club. In 1924 a group of the caricatures was exhibited as part of his first exhibition 'by Courtesy of the Committee of the Yorick Club, with "Comments by an Old Member".'

Sime was a popular member of the club. After his wedding, he intended to live in Scotland, and resigned from the Yorick. The fact that his fellow-members liked him is reflected in the presents they gave him at the time, which were exactly and most sympathetically tailored to his tastes: a richly-bound set of Meredith and a Japanese screen.

* * *

Daldrishaig provided a retreat and therefore satisfied one side of Sime's nature; but Scotland was too far away from London and the stimulus of congenial work and colleagues. For two years he took a studio in the Pheasantry in the King's Road, Chelsea – then still a village whose very name was synonymous with art. In 1903 he arrived at what appeared to be an ideal compromise. He bought an old inn at Worplesdon, a village near Guildford, from which London was readily accessible. He also kept a foothold in London by sharing studios and rooms with friends. One of these studios was at 86 Newman Street, and the use of it came as the result of an imperative suggestion to Josef Holbrooke, in a letter of 4 July 1910: 'Impress upon Johnson the immediate necessity of finding *our* studio. We will draw together the most refreshing set of men who are do-ers to be found in London.' This 'refreshing set' turned out to include, among others, Lord Dunsany.

The Illustrated Books

Lord Dunsany was a central figure in Sime's life, as professional collaborator, patron and friend. They first came together in 1904, when Sime was forty. Dunsany was twenty-six. His family was of Norman descent, his title an Irish one, dating from the fifteenth century. The family had lived in Dunsany Castle for over 700 years. He had been born at Dunstall Priory, 'a small but attractive property' in Kent belonging to his mother and very near to the valley where Samuel Palmer had painted out his intensity of vision in the 1840s. In 1899, after leaving Eton, Dunsany had joined the Coldstream Guards and fought with them in the Boer War. Having inherited his father's title, he was in 1904 attempting to follow him into Parliament, but was unsuccessful.

This was a conventional pattern of life for a young aristocrat of the time. But there was another side to Dunsany. Through his mother he was related to Sir Richard Burton, explorer of little-known lands and translator of *The Arabian Nights*. As a boy he had absorbed the fairy-tales of Hans Christian Andersen and the Authorized Version of the Bible. These ingredients had been working in what Henry James called 'the deep well of unconscious cerebration', reforming into a shape that sought for expression. This expression was stimulated, writes Dunsany in his autobiography, by Jack Hope-Johnstone, who, 'amongst fox-hunting men . . . used to speak to me about such things as books'; and by 'seeing a play at His Majesty's Theatre called "The Darling of the Gods" [by David Belasco]. This play helped to show me that there was a world where boundaries were beyond the furthest fox-hunt and outside political schemes.' So Dunsany sat down and wrote a book – a series of tales – creating his own world far beyond these boundaries.

Having written this book, Dunsany made drawings for it 'but had the sense to realize that far better illustrations might be found. Yet I could only think of two men that I felt I should like to illustrate it, and one of them I knew was dead and I did not know whether the other still lived or not.' The first was Gustave Doré. The second was Sime, who had made copies after Doré while a student. He was presumably tracked down through the publishers of the magazine in whose pages Dunsany had seen his work. 'This remarkable man consented to do me eight illustrations, and I have never seen a black-and-white artist with a more stupendous imagination.'

Although Sime is known as an illustrator, the large bulk of his illustration work for magazines is, if not entirely independent of, only partly dependent on the accompanying text. Writing to Holbrooke in 1911 about a commission, apparently not taken up, to illustrate 'a beastly American poet for many shekels', Sime makes a telling, if cynical, point about one purpose of illustration and the desirability of it to publishers: 'Only the sick need a physician.' But Dunsany's gods and never-never lands, boldly created in a language akin to that of the Authorized Version, would have chimed in with his own growing fascination with 'other worlds than ours'. The texture of Dunsany's language and his kind of humour would have appealed to Sime; as would Dunsany's mastery of implication and suspense. And, more importantly,

Menu-card for the Yorick Club, 1899

Sime was given the same freedom that Rossetti had demanded, as an illustrator, for, as he had put it, 'allegorizing on one's own hook'. 'Of course', Dunsany goes on to say in *Patches of Sunlight*, 'the gods and heavens that he drew for me were totally different from anything that I had imagined, but I knew that it would be impossible to catch Sime's Pegasus and drive it exactly along some track that I had travelled myself, and that if it were possible, it could only be done by clipping its wings. So I left Mr. Sime to do exactly as he liked.'

The first product of this ideal relationship between author and illustrator was published by Elkin Mathews in 1905: '*The Gods of Pegāna* by Lord Dunsany, with eight illustrations by S. H. Sime'. This rather insubstantial pageant – the short pieces it contains are prose-poems rather than tales – creates a dream-world with a vague affinity to that of Greek mythology, equally vaguely akin to Wagner's re-creation of legend, but essentially individual. 'Lord Dunsany has succumbed to the fascination of composing a new theology' wrote the *Daily Telegraph* reviewer.

The book's reception was generally good; Sime's part in its creation was recognized and praised. The *Daily Telegraph* review continued: 'If the result had merely been the fantastic and finely imagined illustrations evoked from the sombre pencil of Mr. S. H. Sime it would have been sufficient . . .' The *Pall Mall Gazette* gave as its opinion that 'Never, we think, has Mr. Sime shown such high imaginative qualities as in these drawings.'

Some of these same drawings appeared under a headline couched in much less reticent language: 'Fantastic New Drawings by S. H. Sime, the Greatest Living Imaginative Artist.' The cutting from the *American-Journal-Examiner* was understandably preserved by Sime, and is now in a folder at Worplesdon. It lacks a date, but is 'copyright 1906'. Thorpe records that in 1905 Sime 'went to the United States, on the invitation of William Randolph Hearst, the American newspaper magnate'; and that Sime had already done some illustrations for Hearst; but it would seem likely that it was Dunsany's *The Gods of Pegana* that caught the attention of that remarkable figure.

The Hearst connection was short-lived. Offered a retainer of £800 a year and the publication of any drawings he made, Sime nevertheless came back to England after six months.

Soon after his return from America, Sime was at work on the next Dunsany book, *Time and The Gods*, published, with ten illustrations, by Heinemann in 1906. Further collections of 'tales' appeared at two-yearly intervals: 1908, 1910, 1912; the last, with six plates, in 1916. There is a sort of progression. Time immemorial – passing time is always the enemy – succeeds 'before the Beginning'; kings and warriors join the cast alongside gods; some tales have their origins in a possible past, even a possible present; ordinary mortals appear, except they are not or-dinary, even if they sell insurance instead of more usually being human voyagers – highwaymen, sailors or gypsies. Yet these books form a whole. 'Come with me, ladies and gentlemen who are in any wise weary of London', Dunsany prefaced *The Book of Wonder*, 'come with me: and those that tire at all of the world we know: for we have new worlds here'. Xanadu was a new world created during the 'renascence of wonder' a century earlier, and for Dunsany, *Kubla Khan* was 'the horn in the dark'. 'That poem of Coleridge calls forth the imagination to leave all the haunts it knows and to fare forth into far strange lands . . . the spirit of Coleridge travels to look for magic and wonder.' He could have been writing about himself; and about the artist he had chosen as collaborator.

As there was a progression in Dunsany's writing so there was in Sime's art. *Time and The Gods* shows author and artist on much more familiar terms with their creations than they had been in *The Gods of Pegana*; in pictures like 'Lo! the Gods.' and 'Yazun is God' awe has given place to amusement. Everything is seen in sharper focus yet the aura of wonder is sustained, nowhere more eloquently than in 'The Dirge of Shimono Kani'. So far Dunsany had been occupied with the gods alone but in *The Sword of Welleran* he moved to new worlds, and the response of his illustrator was both more literal and less certain. Against the success of such drawings as 'Welleran and the Sword of Welleran' and 'Even I too!' (as sympathetic an interpretation of Dunsany's words as Sime ever achieved) must be set others which do less to enhance the text. But Sime returned to his best form in the next book. *A Dreamer's Tales* contains some of the most lyrical passages in all Dunsany's *oeuvre*: 'the old and holy figure of Romance, cloaked even to the face, comes down out of hilly woodlands' evoked from Sime the most poetic of all his pictures. Scarcely less captivating is 'We would gallop through Africa'. After *The Book of Wonder*, in which the collaboration of Sime and Dunsany reached its apogee, *Tales of Wonder* is a sad come-down. It was published in 1916, a time when 'the edge of the world' was of less interest to most people than the world in which they hoped to survive.

The partnership of Dunsany and Sime was rare in the history of the illustrated book. At one stage Dunsany completely reversed the normal order of things. 'I found Mr Sime one day, in his strange house at Worplesdon, complaining that editors did not offer him very suitable subjects for illustration; so I said: "Why not do any pictures you like, and I will write stories explaining them, which may add a little to their mystery?"' If these words – apparently self-contradictory – were indeed Dunsany's own exactly, they were perceptively well chosen. Sime's chief desire was to make his pictures ever 'more mysterious'. This invitation resulted in *The Book of Wonder*: Sime and Dunsany were so much in harmony that the reversal of roles is not immediately apparent. In fact, Sime presented Dunsany with drawings that were particularly over-elaborate, and Dunsany distilled elements from them to make stories. Both men were at times given to excessive elaboration – clutter is too coarse a word for it, but only just – and this gave rise to a risk of wrecking the whole effect, perhaps by just one detail. Sime's finest achievements lay in those drawings that contain the essence, and not the paraphernalia, of magic and mystery: such drawings as 'Hish' and the frontispiece to *The King of Elfland's Daughter*.

After *Tales of Wonder*, Sime's collaboration, where it continued at all, is reduced to a frontispiece. Thorpe suggests that this may have been due to economies in publishing after the war, but it also coincides with Dunsany's expansion of his tales into novel-length books, in which much of the expansion is descriptive writing. The narrative line, picaresque in *Rodriguez*, is stretched in both *The King of Elfland's Daughter* and *The Blessing of Pan*. The stories that form the basis of these last two books are 'illustrated' by Dunsany himself: in words; and often to great effect. 'Lirazel, the fairy-child, returned to Elfland, kneels before her father's throne in the hall that was built of moonlight, dreams, music and mirage.' Sime's frontispiece, though an accurate description of a passage of the book, nevertheless is out of key with it as a whole, like his very first published drawing for Dunsany. The frontispiece to *The Gods of Pegana* is in Beardsley style and effete; that to *The King of Elfland's Daughter* is very dark in mood, despairing; more appropriate to, say, Nietzsche's lines 'O Man take heed, what does the dark midnight say' than to Dunsany's shimmering fairyland.

There is a distinct change in Dunsany's imaginative writing after the war. The forces that lie beyond 'the fields we know' – a favourite phrase – removed and remote in the early tales, take over in those two books, written in the twenties, that together mark his greatest achievement. In *The King of Elfland's Daughter*, a medieval town is swept over and enclosed by 'the bright line', the curtain containing fairyland; in *The Blessing of Pan* a Kentish village is invaded and captured by Pan, embodiment of an older faith, an ascendancy that the author clearly supports. Sime was completely in sympathy with Dunsany's wish to withdraw, if only in the alternative world of the imagination, from the 'real world' of the twentieth century.

Dunsany not only thought of Sime as a genius but liked him personally, inviting him to stay on at least three occasions and visiting him at Worplesdon. Lady Dunsany warmed to him immediately. When he first went to Dunsany Castle in October 1910 she wrote in her diary:

Mr Sime stayed here last week and left last Monday 17th. He is *very* nice, most interesting and amusing and the nice kind of guest who likes doing and seeing anything and is perfectly happy sketching or reading or talking when there is nothing to see or do. He started life as a miner but the only trace left is in his features which are rough-looking – his head is magnificent, his manners perfect, his conversation that of a scholar and a philosopher, his interests and knowledge vast and varied. Mr Russell [A.E.] came for Sunday and the two made great friends and sat up nearly all night together.

It would seem that, as a book illustrator, Sime needed the encouragement of friendship, for the illustrations he provided for Arthur Machen do not compare with the best of his work for Dunsany.

The recorded connection between Sime and Machen is limited to two frontispieces. Of all contemporary writers, Machen must have had a strong appeal for Sime. He certainly provided what would have been ideal passages for Sime to illustrate: Dyson's words at the end of the prologue to *The Three Impostors*, for example. (This book so terrified Conan Doyle that he could not sleep after reading it.)

I yield to fantasy [Dyson pronounces roundly]; I cannot withstand the influence of the grotesque. Here, where all is falling into dimness and dissolution, and we walk in cedarn gloom, and the very air of heaven goes mouldering to the lungs, I cannot remain commonplace. I look at that deep glow on the panes and the house lies all enchanted; that very room, I tell you, is within all blood and fire.

What a Sime could have come out of that! But all we have are frontispieces to *The House of Souls*, 1906, and to *The Hill of Dreams*, 1907.

Caricature of Lord Howard de Walden and Josef Holbrooke

Theatre Design

'For though new streams set in over the broken lands and all our shores are strange; though the dynasties are gone and honour seems lost under the queer jetsam of these tides: yet Nodens dreams on.' So ends the preface to *The Cauldron of Annwn*, written by Thomas Evelyn Ellis (Lord Howard de Walden), one of the friends most crucial to Sime's career. The extract shows the preoccupation with mystery and romance which Howard de Walden shared with Sime, Machen and Dunsany.

In a collection of essays published in English in 1902, fittingly entitled *The Buried Temple*, Maeterlinck wrote: 'It is not unreasonable to believe that the paramount interest of life, all that is truly lofty and remarkable in the destiny of man, reposes almost entirely in the mystery that surrounds us; in the two mysteries, it may be, that are mightiest, most dreadful of all – fatality and death.' It was this mystery that the three writers and their 'illustrator' were preoccupied with, and it is a sense of this mystery that pervades their work, whether it is set in imagined heavens, 'another part of the forest', the dark streets of London or in hidden valleys where old legends and antique faiths still hold sway.

Howard de Walden was a reticent grandee and polymath, a man of great wealth and estates, a figure in society, accomplished sportsman and traveller.

Costume design for Ibsen's *The Pretenders*, 1913

He was also a poet and lavish patron of the arts. Through his connection with the Theatre Royal, Haymarket, he played a part in the growth of the London theatre during the Edwardian period. In association with Herbert Trench, also a poet, he put on Maeterlinck's *The Blue Bird* in 1909 and Ibsen's *The Pretenders* in 1913, both with designs by Sime.

Lord Howard had met the composer Josef Holbrooke at a performance of the latter's symphonic poem, *Apollo and the Seaman*. In 1908 they began work on an ambitious project. Howard de Walden had come across a copy of *The Mabinogion*, Welsh legends translated by Lady Charlotte Guest. He 'fell into the fascination of these strange old stories' and 'wanted to write the tale of Bronwen, daughter of Llyr, once more'. With Josef Holbrooke as his composer, he turned the legends into the libretto of a trilogy of operas, or music-dramas. Sime was engaged as the designer.

The second part of the trilogy was published first; the score of *Dylan*, elaborately printed and with a cover by Sime, was published in 1910. The first part, *The Children of Don*, was published, in a similar format, in 1912, and was staged in June of that year at the London Opera House. It had three performances, the first two conducted by Arthur Nikisch, the third by Holbrooke himself. *Dylan* was put on at Drury Lane by Thomas Beecham in 1914. The third part, *Bronwen*, was not performed until 1929, when the Carl Rosa Company staged it at Huddersfield.

The thought and energy that went into the creation of this great effort is apparent from the letters from Sime to Holbrooke and Howard de Walden that have survived. From these we see that Sime did not regard his role as limited to designer; but he did careful homework, researching information and illustrations in order to get the details of costume and furniture right, and went to Stonehenge with Holbrooke. In order to get the full Druidical effect, they saw it by moonlight. 'I never saw imaginative mind expressed in such awful shapes of matter', Sime wrote afterwards to Holbrooke.

'The Eminent Artist, Mr. S. H. Sime', as he appeared on the programme cover of *The Children of Don*, and Holbrooke worked hard, but there was no commercial pressure. Indeed the project introduced them both to an agreeable world. Howard de Walden's home, the 'medieval Castle of Chirk', and his London residence, Seaford House, were open to them. There were visits to Shona, his private island, and even a Mediterranean cruise on the R.Y.S. *Calysta*. Lady Howard de Walden recalls these days in her memoirs, 'The rehearsals were enthralling and entertaining. Arguments about lighting, battles over advantageous cuts, or Beecham, baton in right hand stroking his tiny pointed beard upwards with the back of his small left hand, and loudly drawling "give it hell boys!"'

This was in June 1914. Among the splendid, rolling lines of the libretto of *Dylan*, some words of Gwydion's may well have rung with ominous appropriateness:

. . . there breathes
About me menace of dire things to come.
Great beings watch, and a low distant drum
Thunders for change.

* * *

On 4 August Britain declared war on Germany. Sime described the scene around him:

Worplesdon is a seething mass of ribald soldiery – about 12,000 of 'em dossing on the common. They cluster round the village pub in the twilight like swarms of bees and I hear the continuous tramp of feet and the sound of martial voices saying 'Hello Gertie' and 'Is that you Maud?'

Heroics were not in the line of a man familiar at an early age with unpleasant and dangerous conditions: 'A neighbour has been awarded the G.P.O. or something and the village is delirious'. His movements in wartime were restricted, but he told Howard de Walden:

I am ermite by no choice. The Kaiser has filched my spare cash. The railway gods have stuck up the fare on me, I've sold my motorbike, and I have some books I want to read – then of course I keep on doing a bit of painting.

He had to leave Worplesdon for a short time when he was called up in July 1918. He wrote to Howard de Walden:

My army complications are not of my seeking, tho' I don't worry about it. An artist at work is the most irritating thing your beef-witted patriot can ever see. Let us make him do something of national importance. So I must sally forth and swab out the colonel's spittoon.

Sime went off to war 'not in shining armour and with glittering sword, but with a slop pail and a tin of polishing paste'. He developed a duodenal ulcer and was invalided out on Armistice Day. During his convalescence in Worplesdon he wrote again to Howard de Walden:

The village inn is too far off for my energies yet so I can't send you any momentous news. Art is in abeyance but I still have some courage in that delusion – although Fleet St. seems to loom ahead as my only hope. Peace has its defeats as well as war.

The Exhibitions of 1924 and 1927

After Sime's connection with the Royal Society of British Artists had ceased, his work had been seen in public only once, at the Baillie Gallery in 1907, when he had shown a group of caricatures in a mixed exhibition. Since then he had been occupied in other directions. During the war he had become obsessed by the Apocalypse, and was painting to please himself. 'My oil stunts are getting more and more addled', he wrote to Holbrooke on 10 October 1916, 'and I like 'em better and better although they look somewhat like undigested poetry.'

Cover design for the score of *Bronwen*, opera by Josef Holbrooke, published 1922

On 12 February 1923 a serious decision is conveyed to Howard de Walden in a letter. 'Hist! I'm going to have a show. That last infirmity of senile kind.'

His illustration work had thinned to a trickle and, now nearly sixty, he had no pension to look forward to. So hard necessity, 'the furtherance of sordid ends', as Sime put it, prompted an exhibition, although 'exaltation at the giddy prospect don't sweep over me in turbulent waves'.

Lord Dunsany and Lord Howard de Walden made loans, and Macfall wrote a breathless foreword to the catalogue. The exhibition was held at the St George's Gallery, George Street, in 1924. The gallery was next door to the church in which George Meredith was married for the first time, a fact that would have appealed to Sime.

Of the seventy-eight items in the show, forty-two were lent, though Sime, writing to thank Lord Howard for his co-operation, says, 'all that I would borrow is just enough to pad out my leanness'.

'It ain't my show – it's his'n. He gets the ha-pence and I get the kix,' said Sime, referring to the gallery owner, Arthur Howell. Despite this, Sime stood to gain financially by a successful show and, according to Lady Dunsany, it did go well. She writes in her diary for 22 June 1924, 'Sime was here for two nights, in spite of his philosophy he was, I am glad to say, human enough not to hide his pleasure over the success of his picture show. And when he is pleased nobody can be more charming.'

The exhibition covered the range of Sime's creative output; this was the first time his work had been seen in the round. Macfall, in the catalogue, says, 'It is almost unthinkable that the art of one of the men of genius of our generation is to be seen in its fuller significance for the first time by the public today.'

The exhibition was extensively reviewed. *Colour Magazine* thought it was 'probably one of the outstanding events of the art season'. The *Illustrated London News* and the *Studio* both did Sime proud with double-page spreads. The latter called the show 'a very remarkable gathering,' 'a demonstration of the powers of an artist of exceptional individuality and very great capacity and possessed of an amazing fertility of imagination,' But the *Spectator* gave the show only two lines. 'Mr Sime's work is suggestive of the attempt on the part of a bad poet to express himself in a medium whose difficulties have been underestimated. His symbolism would have appeared better in print.'

The longest and perhaps the most carefully considered reaction to Sime's work took up nearly a page in the *New Statesman*. The reviewer, J. F. Holms, wrote: 'He happens to have been born an extremely capable draughtsman with a genuine sense of colour; but in a moment of confusion the fairy's hand shook, and she dropped him, to complete the gift, not a painter's imagination but a writer's.' Holms uses the word 'German' frequently and his review throws a strong, if slanted, light across Sime's work, picking out in detail its gothic and grotesque elements. 'Here are the terrors of nature, the vast and cloudy abysses, the dream landscapes, the trolls, monsters and hobgoblins, the neglect of all humanity except the conventionally heroic or symbolic, the insistence on cosmic allegory, and the lack of fundamental design.'

The fact that the exhibition had been a success outweighed such reviews and, three years later, Howell put on a second Sime exhibition. But this show was a thinner repetition of the first. The caricature of Sime by Max Beerbohm which had been used in the first catalogue was used again; there were no paintings of any stature; the Yorick Club caricatures were replaced by caricatures of Worplesdon locals, unlikely to appeal to a London audience. Although *Apollo* was enthusiastic, the *Studio* found the show 'a little disappointing'.

After this exhibition Sime's withdrawal from the world became virtually complete.

Later Years at Worplesdon

'So I found this old public-house which was going cheap and here I am,' Sime told the *Liverpool Echo* in 1927.

'This old public house' was Crown Cottage at Worplesdon. Sime probably chose Worplesdon because it was the home of his friend Duncan Tovey. Tovey's wife, Joan, was to become the first curator of the Sime Memorial Gallery. Crown Cottage is an old red brick house close to the village green. Sime had some alterations done and opened up a large living-room. Round the walls were many of Sime's own pictures, mainly unframed, and prints by Hokusai and Hiroshige in ebony frames; eastern *objets d'art* were on the shelves and tables; in one corner stood a harp.

Sime converted the old stable into a large studio for his wife and himself. On the walls were prints of the work of artists Sime admired, including Goya, Piranesi, Meryon, Seymour Hayden, F. L. Griggs, and his friend Augustus John, with whom he had shared a mountain retreat in Wales for a time before the war.

From the beginning of his partnerships with Dunsany in 1904 and with Howard de Walden in about 1909 Sime had been busy, or as busy as he wanted to be, until the war curtailed these activities. After the war he spent quite a lot of time loafing around.

'Art' he wrote, in the preface to the catalogue of his 1927 exhibition, 'is great fun'; yet his attitude to it was curiously ambivalent. As early as 1908 he told the interviewer for the *Strand Magazine* that he had 'acquired a small competence and don't now depend on his (the man in the street's) suffrage . . . I like to draw things which tickle my fancy – but let me be quite frank with you; I really think farming or sailoring better occupations for a grown man.' To Dunsany he once remarked, 'After the age of forty no man ought to do anything but stretch out his hand for food.'

Yet he did spend long hours in the studio, often working from 'closing time' until the small hours of the morning. These were the hours when he wrestled with the visions of St John in the Book of Revelation and painted his own visions of the Apocalypse. Or he would work over prints of his old magazine illustrations and caricatures, make abstract designs based on oriental patterns, or paint delicate pictures inspired by the random fall of matches on a table.

Sime's painting in oil and watercolour was of the greatest importance to him; of that there can be no doubt. To him it transcended any reputation he may have gained as a contributor to the magazines or the illustrator of Dunsany. Yet for us it is extremely difficult to have an opinion of its merit. The whereabouts of the early pictures exhibited at the R.B.A. is unknown and only a handful of his later pictures have been traced outside the collection at Worplesdon. Of these later pictures, the original version of 'Wild Beast Wood', rightly called his 'masterpiece', was reproduced in colour in 'Masterpieces of Modern Art', *Colour Magazine*, 1926, with the comment:

'Philosophers and writers on the arts from the time of the ancients to the present day have speculated on the proper

'St John at Patmos', woodcut for *Form*, New Series, 1921

treatment of the 'horrible' in art. Mr S. H. Sime has methods of his own whereby with a touch of sly humour the horrors he presents to us are made bearable and indeed attractive. Incidentally, he is a most skilful draughtsman, as can be seen here in the clever treatment of the trees.'

The Worplesdon collection contains a number of paintings that were worked over by Mary Sime after her husband's death, as well as some pictures that are unfinished. For these reasons generalization is dangerous but it can be said that the watercolours are more impressive than the oils, the nature of water-colour militating against second thoughts. Those oils that we have seen generally show Sime at his worst; trying to become 'ever more mysterious' too often resulted in becoming ever more muddled.

Sime was often visited by Adrian Beach, a painter living in Worplesdon, who records that he usually had twenty or thirty pictures in progress at the same time. The young Beach was given the benefit of much advice: Sime counselled him against becoming an artist or, if he was determined to do so, against attending an art school. Beach came to have a great affection and respect for Sime, which even survived the occasion when, as a student at the Royal College of Art, he showed Sime the painting that had won for him the Prix de Rome. 'Cover it in chrome yellow and start again', was Sime's advice.

Another man who visited Sime at Worplesdon and was much impressed was Desmond Coke. In his book, *Confessions of an Incurable Collector*, 1928, he tells of his experience buying the painting, 'Wild Beast Wood', from this man who was 'alleged to be so difficult' and concludes:

Sime, however, more than most alleged 'geniuses' whom I have met, has something of the real spark in him . . . his shattering conversation, his knowledge of the paints that he himself mixes, with the loving care of an Old Master, in his rustic cottage/studio: his recondite knowledge of the Apocalypse; and above all his small output and contempt for fame. He has only to die and the inevitable Memorial Exhibition will introduce an era of Sime-hunting and big prices. I hope, however, that he will not hurry.

The friends that Sime had made in his early days in London seem to have played no part in his life at Worplesdon. We hear no more of Arnold Golsworthy, Arthur Lawrence, Frank and Walter Emanuel, or of the members of the Yorick Club. But his friendship and companionship were highly prized. Augustus John came down from London, and the painter Walter G. Johnson, who lived at Guildford, was a constant visitor and drinking companion. The Dunsanys came to see him, as did Howard de Walden and Josef Holbrooke, with their families. However, the men Sime saw most were the patrons of the New Inn at Worplesdon.

The New Inn, now demolished, was an attractive three-storey building with an eighteenth-century façade. Mrs Wadey, the landlord's daughter, recalls Sime well and describes how he was at the New Inn every evening without fail, drinking whisky, and often at lunch-time too. He never said much but was 'very good-natured'. He sometimes entered into political discussions, advancing radical views quite unconnected with party politics, which he despised, and gave the impression of arguing for the fun of it. He often uttered grave warnings against the 'Yellow Peril'.

'Wild Beast Wood', oil-painting, reproduced in 'Masterpieces of Modern Art', *Colour Magazine*, 1926

He always wore the same old blue suit and stood in the same place at the bar, opposite a long mirror in which he could see most of the customers, who were, in the main, local working men or tradesmen. He was making mental notes of their appearance, for his caricatures. Most of these were very popular with the victims; if anyone objected, Sime gave him the drawing to destroy if he wished. The rest were given to the landlord and hung in the bar. They are now in the Sime Memorial Gallery. Sime wrote an article about them in the *Evening News*, May 1926.

After he left the pub, Sime often went for long walks in the countryside around before returning to his studio to paint or read late into the night. Books were a passion with Sime. 'I owe everything to omnivorous and indiscriminate reading', he told the interviewer in the *Strand Magazine* in 1908. 'If I mention Poe, Heine, De Quincey, it will give you some indication of my preferences in literature. And Meredith – above all, Meredith.' Frank Harris was amazed at his knowledge of William Blake and quoted a letter from Sime about Blake's significance in *Contemporary Portraits* to show both the depth of his thought and his gift for exposition. He read, apparently, eight to ten books a week.

Sime was in no sense a bibliophile, but he had a fine collection of Blake, including several rare works. Most of his books were sold to a local auctioneer after he died; had his library survived intact we should most likely have discovered in it many books on mysticism and esoteric knowledge. Sime was deeply versed in the *Cabala*, the *Upanishads* and the writings of Jacob Boehme. There may, too, have been some scientific works. Sime had a telescope through which he gazed at the stars and a microscope that was trained on various forms of insect life, some of which appear in his drawings. He conducted experiments with electricity; in the course of an experiment with a primitive chemistry set he nearly blew the roof off his studio.

After these night-time activities, Sime rose very late and his first excursion, as often as not, was to the post office to place his bets on the day's races. He invented a 'system' (recalled by the present Lord Dunsany) which, with typical cynicism, was based on the fallibility of racing correspondents, and he was much given to expounding its operation at the New Inn. Those who followed it did not prosper.

Most of Sime's letters to Howard de Walden are so luxuriant in language and facetious in tone – Sime in the role of court jester – that it is difficult to discover his true feelings; yet latterly they give an impression of melancholia and in the 1930s he referred to himself on two occasions as 'decrepit'.

His marriage apparently brought him no consolation. They had no children. Mary Sime, regarded as the local beauty, was shy and introverted. She shared many of her husband's interests in art, music and the exploration of esoteric knowledge, but not his social instincts. She was highly strung, touchy and often in pain from arthritis. Her contacts with the outside world seem to have come mainly from a dancing class she ran for local girls, for whom she designed pretty costumes, and from the occasional commission to paint portrait miniatures. She guarded her husband's privacy closely and the home atmosphere was claustrophobic, from which Sime found partial release at the pub.

Sime's finances during this period remain something of a mystery. During the last twenty years of his life he must have earned very little. He sold a number of pictures at the London exhibitions, did a few magazine illustrations, drawings for Dunsany, designs for furniture and decorations commissioned by Howard de Walden. He had inherited a handsome sum and there must have been some of it left after the purchase and conversion of Crown Cottage, and the payment of debts incurred over the *Idler*. But, even if he invested the remainder, was it really a 'competence'? It is more than likely that Howard de Walden helped him from time to time. We know that Lord Dunsany wrote to Sir Kenneth Clark in 1940, when Sime had been very ill, enquiring if it would be possible to obtain some sort of pension for him.

Sime died on 22 May 1941, and was buried in Worplesdon churchyard. A rough block of granite, now obscured by undergrowth, marks his grave. It is laconically inscribed, 'Sidney Herbert Sime 1941'.

The two peers who had played such an important part in Sime's life wrote typically generous and loyal letters to his widow. Howard de Walden sent her a cheque which he hoped she would 'accept as either a loan or part payment for some little memento of your husband which you might care to let me have later on'. A few months later he was asking if he might try to arrange an exhibition of Sime's work. 'I don't like the idea of his being forgotten only to be rediscovered a hundred years hence' – and in June 1942 he was hoping that a little exhibition could be held at the Tate Gallery 'if enough good specimens could be collected . . . I am determined that he should be recognized in spite of himself'.

Dunsany was abroad at the time of Sime's death, but on his return wrote in March 1942: 'I have often expressed in conversations, in lectures and in my autobiography and elsewhere, my admiration for his genius, and I feel now that the world has lost a unique character, a loss that is quite irreplaceable.' He also sent Mary Sime a cheque on account of a purchase.

The epilogue is sad. There was no exhibition at the Tate Gallery, or anywhere else. In 1949 Mary Sime, by then a cripple living in squalor, died in tragic circumstances. In her will she bequeathed all Sime's pictures that remained with her to the Trustees of the Worplesdon Memorial Hall for the creation of a Sime Memorial Gallery – which she endowed with the proceeds of the sale of Crown Cottage. Mrs Tovey assembled the exhibits, catalogued them, and, helped by Adrian Beach, arranged them with discrimination. The gallery was opened in 1956 and, after an initial stir of local interest, is now visited by about six people each year.

Conclusion

'A genius whose stupendous imagination has passed across our time little more noticed by most people than the shadow of a bird passing over the lawn would be noticed by most of a tennis party.' So Dunsany described Sime in the *Fortnightly Review* the year after his death.

How was it that Sime was so neglected?

Part of the answer is that it was a self-inflicted wound. Desmond Coke has recorded that Sime 'told enquiring dealers to go Hell' and that he had the reputation of being 'very difficult'. A reviewer of the 1924 exhibition described it as 'the first he has permitted'. Some of this defiance sprang from a natural arrogance, but some was inspired by self-doubt, the fear that his pictures were not wanted. 'Painting – that solemn but amusing tomfoolery – I have put by me', he told Howard de Walden in the early Twenties, 'by reason of the contemptuous horror aroused in spectators of it.'

Moreover he was lazy. After the activity of the Nineties, he actually completed very little. 'I grow more and more fond of loafing', he told Hannen Swaffer in 1922. He painted when it pleased him and he painted for himself; seldom satisfied with his efforts to make his pictures more mysterious, he left many unfinished at his death.

Dunsany could extol Sime's 'stupendous imagination' because his castle was adorned with Sime's original drawings. Most people were ignorant of Sime's existence on account of what Coke called his 'small output and contempt for fame'.

In another sense Sime was neglected because his temper ran counter to the aesthetics of the age. The artists of the Nineties were individuals. As the twentieth century progressed, so artists tended to combine; they adopted theories, joined movements, issued manifestoes. Above all, they became serious and socially conscious. It did not suit Sime any more than it suited his friend Augustus John. Isolated at Worplesdon, Sime turned a deaf ear to the calls for 'significant form'.

Even as an illustrator he did not fit in. He was (whatever his own opinion) pre-eminently a black-and-white artist and achieved his success in the Nineties, heyday of the black-and-white men. In the following decade, most of the magazines turned to photography, reserving space for those comic artists who left no doubt about their intentions. Book publishers went for colour; it was the era of the 'Gift Book'. Sime could not compete with Arthur Rackham, Edmund Dulac, Kay Nielsen, Harry Clarke, E. J. Detmold, Willy Pogany or the Robinsons. They had a capacity to charm the eye; his ability was to slide into the subconscious.

Essentially Sime was neglected because his art was not explicable. Many would have agreed with Bernard Muddiman who, in his book, *The Men of the Nineties*, praised its 'marvellous suggestive power'. But what was its message? Was Sime serious, or was he playing the Fool?

A good instance of this confusion concerns Sime's illustrations of the after-life, 'Ye Shades'. Frank Emanuel, writing about them in the *Magazine of Art*, 1904, said, 'the idea of using his art as a means to point salutary morals was either absent or of mere incidental import to him.' Holbrook Jackson, on the other hand, rated the moral content high in his book, *The Eighteen Nineties*, published in 1913. 'His satires of Heaven and Hell, funny as they are, do not end as jokes. He sees in these popular conceptions of the hereafter mere substitutes for thought and imagination and courageous living.'

It was no good asking Sime to help. His only object was to add to the mystery. His letters plumb no depths either, for he wished to entertain his correspondents and splashed about in words like a child at the seaside, kicking up spray for the fun of it.

So it was not surprising that Sime was disregarded, and there is no point in trying to atone for this by constructing a serious rationale for his art. The man with the scrubbing brush and bucket is bound to wander through. The only thing to do is to look closely at his best drawings and let imagination take over.

Relishing mysteriousness and obscurity for their own sakes, Sime did not want his pictures to be explicable. Like Meredith, he knew:

Ah, what a dusty answer gets the soul
When hot for certainties in this our life!

But he could laugh not only at the fact that men for ages had been 'hot' for answers to the old questions, but that he shared this concern. Even his respect was expressed sardonically.

In 1911 he wrote to Josef Holbrooke: 'An enterprising bloke has asked me to make a large number of drawings for a costly and ornate volume of Edgar Allan Poe. I am philandering with the project not feeling quite equal to my author. You see, I am looking forward to meeting Poe in Hell and I am loth to do anything that would embarrass the encounter.'

Bibliography

All publishers in London unless otherwise stated.

BOOKS ILLUSTRATED BY SIDNEY SIME

Death and the Woman by Arnold Golsworthy. Lawrence Greening 1898.
Cover design.

Fancy Free by Eden Phillpotts. Methuen 1901.
One pen and ink illustration – 'The Zagabog'.

The Gods of Pegana by Lord Dunsany. Elkin Mathews 1905.
2nd ed. Pegana Press 1911. 3rd ed. Elkin Mathews 1919.
Eight illustrations in photogravure.

The House of Souls by Arthur Machen. Grant Richards 1906.
Photogravure frontispiece and designs on upper cover and spine.

Time and The Gods by Lord Dunsany. Heinemann 1906.
2nd ed. G. P. Putnam 1923.
Large paper edition of 250 copies signed by the author and with each plate signed by artist. G. P. Putnam 1922.
Ten full-page illustrations.

The Hill of Dreams by Arthur Machen. Grant Richards 1907.
Photogravure frontispiece.

The Sword of Welleran by Lord Dunsany. George Allen and Sons 1908.
Ten full-page monochrome illustrations (one reproduced from *The Idler*, December 1899).

The Ghost Pirates by William Hope Hodgson. Stanley Paul and Co. 1909.
Frontispiece.

A Dreamer's Tales by Lord Dunsany. George Allen and Sons 1910.
Nine full-page monochrome illustrations.

The Book of Wonder by Lord Dunsany. Heinemann 1912.
2nd ed. Elkin Mathews 1919.
Ten full-page monochrome illustrations (previously published in *The Sketch*, December 1910 and January-March 1911).

Tales of Wonder by Lord Dunsany. Elkin Mathews 1916.
2nd ed. Elkin Mathews 1917.
Six full-page monochrome illustrations (previously published in *The Sketch*, May and June 1914 under the title of 'The Last Book of Wonder').

The Chronicles of Rodriguez by Lord Dunsany. G. P. Putnam, 1st ed. February 1922; 2nd ed. March 1922.
Large paper edition of 500 copies signed by the author and the artist. G. P. Putnam 1922.
Photogravure frontispiece.

Bogey Beasts. Jingles, etc. by Sidney H. Sime. Music by Josef Holbrooke.
Goodwin and Tabb N. D. [1923].
Fifteen full-page monochrome illustrations.

The King of Elfland's Daughter by Lord Dunsany. Heinemann 1924.
Large paper edition of 250 copies signed by author and artist. G. P. Putnam 1924.
Photogravure frontispiece.

The Blessing of Pan by Lord Dunsany. G. P. Putnam 1927.
Frontispiece. (Book dedicated to S. H. Sime.)

My Talks with Dean Spanley by Lord Dunsany. Heinemann 1936.
Frontispiece.

MAGAZINES WITH ORIGINAL CONTRIBUTIONS BY SIDNEY SIME

Black and White. Title page for Xmas No. 1899

The Boy's Own Paper. Wood engraved full-page. March 1893.

The Butterfly, New Series. Many illustrations between March 1899 and January 1900.

Eureka. Many illustrations between July 1897 and April 1898. Also in *Yule-Tide Tales*, the Christmas Annual for 1897.

Form, New Series. No. 1, October 1921. Woodcut: 'St John at Patmos'.

The Graphic. Coloured illustrations in Xmas No. 1926.

The Idler. Many illustrations between February 1896 and January 1901.

The Illustrated London News, November 1892; Xmas No. 1920; November 1922; Xmas No. 1922; June 1924; Xmas No. 1925; Xmas No. 1926; Xmas No. 1931; Xmas No. 1932.

The Ludgate. Seven illustrations in 1891 and 1892; fourteen illustrations in New Series, 1897 and 1898.

The Minster, Vol. 3, New Series, January, February and March 1896.

The Pall Mall Magazine. Many illustrations between January 1899 and April 1906.

Pick-Me-Up. Many illustrations between August 1895 and December 1899.

Punch. Two cartoons in 1902.

The Sketch, May 1897; Xmas Supplement December 1903; July–September and Xmas No. 1904; January, April–June 1905; April, November 1906; March–May, December 1910; January–March 1911; May, June 1914.

The Strand Magazine, July, August, October, December 1905; October 1908; December 1910.

The Tatler, August 1901; August 1902; August 1903; January 1905; January 1906. Theatrical caricatures June 1902–May 1904.

The Unicorn. Full-page illustration September 1905.

Note. A full list of Sidney Sime's illustrations in *Pick-Me-Up*, *The Idler*, *The Butterfly* and *The Pall Mall Magazine* can be found in George Locke's *From an Ultimate Dim Thule*. Ferret Fantasy 1973.

REFERENCES TO SIDNEY SIME'S LIFE AND WORK
Listed in chronological order

'Five Black-and-White Artists' by Arthur Girdlestone in *The Windsor Magazine*, December 1897.

'The Apotheosis of the Grotesque'. Mr S. H. Sime interviewed by Arthur Lawrence in *The Idler*, January 1898.

Article on Sidney Sime and Max Beerbohm by Arthur Lawrence in *Eureka*, April 1898.

'High Art and High Jinks at "The Langham"' by Arthur Lawrence in *To-Day*, November 1898.

'Some Modern Caricaturists' by P. G. Konody in *The Idler*, February 1899.

'Some Thoughts on the Art of S. H. Sime' by Hal Dane [Haldane Macfall] in *Saint Paul's*, September 1899.

'The Revolving Bookcase' by Richard Le Gallienne in *The Idler*, December 1899.

'Our Graphic Humorists: Sidney Sime' by Frank L. Emanuel in *The Magazine of Art*, February 1904.

'Mr S. H. Sime and his work' by E. S. Valentine in *The Strand Magazine*, October 1908.

The Modern Genius by Haldane Macfall. History of Painting Series. T. C. and E. C. Jack 1911.

The Eighteen Nineties by Holbrook Jackson. Grant Richards 1913.

'Among my Drawings' by Walter Emanuel in *The Strand Magazine*, November 1915.

Contemporary Portraits, Second Series, by Frank Harris. Published by the author, New York 1919.

The Men of the Nineties by Bernard Muddiman. Henry Danielson 1920.

'The Genius of Sidney H. Sime' by Major Haldane Macfall in *The Illustrated London News*, November 1922.

'Sime: the Prophet in Line' by Hannen Swaffer in *The Graphic*, November 1922.

A Story Teller by W. Pett Ridge. Hodder and Stoughton 1923.

Catalogue of Sidney H. Sime's Exhibition at the St George's Gallery, London W1, 1924. Introduction by Haldane Macfall.

Reproduction of 'Wild Beast Wood' in 'Masterpieces of Modern Art', *Colour Magazine*, January 1926.

I Like to Remember by W. Pett Ridge. Hodder and Stoughton 1925.

Article in *The Evening News* by Sidney H. Sime, 27 May 1926.

Catalogue of Sidney H. Sime's Exhibition at the St George's Gallery, London W1, 1927. Foreword by Sidney Sime.

'From Pit Boy to Artist'. Article in *The Liverpool Echo*, 24 June 1927.

Confessions of an Incurable Collector by Desmond Coke. Chapman and Hall 1928.

Frank Harris by A. I. Tobin and Elmer Gertz. Madeleine Mendelsohn, Chicago, Ill. 1931.

English Illustration: The Nineties by James Thorpe. Faber and Faber 1935.

Patches of Sunlight by Lord Dunsany. Heinemann 1938. (There are also references to Sime in Dunsany's two subsequent books of autobiography – *While the Sirens Slept* 1944 and *The Sirens Wake* 1945.)

Let Me Tell You by A. C. R. Carter. Hutchinson 1940.

'Sime' by Lord Dunsany in *The Fortnightly Review*, August 1942.

Aspects of British Art. 'British Cartoonists' by David Low. Collins 1947.

The English Comic Album edited by Leonard Russell and Nicolas Bentley. Michael Joseph 1948.

Article by Martin Gardner in *The Arkham Sampler* (US), Autumn 1949.

An Irish Portrait by Paul Henry. Batsford 1951.

Pages from my Life by Margherita Lady Howard de Walden. Sidgwick and Jackson 1965.

The Art Nouveau Book in Britain by John Russell Taylor. Methuen 1966.

Catalogue of the Aubrey Beardsley Exhibition at the Victoria and Albert Museum, London 1966, by Brian Reade and Frank Dickinson.

Lord Dunsany. A biography by Mark Amory. Collins 1972.

From an Ultimate Dim Thule by George Locke. Ferret Fantasy 1973.

Beasts that Might Have Been by S. H. Sime. Ferret Fantasy 1974.

Augustus John. A biography by Michael Holroyd, vol. 2. Heinemann 1975.

'The Fantasy World of Sidney Sime' by John Lewis in *The Saturday Book*, No. 34. Hutchinson 1975.

The Land of Dreams by George Locke. Ferret Fantasy 1975.

Fantasy: Book Illustration 1860–1920 by Brigid Peppin. Studio Vista 1975.

The Illustrator and the Book in England 1790–1914 by Gordon Ray. Oxford University Press 1976.

Sidney H. Sime, Master of Fantasy by Paul W. Skeeters. Ward Ritchie Press, Pasadena, Calif. 1978.

Note. This list excludes mentions of Sidney Sime's pictures exhibited at the Royal Society of British Artists and reviews of his two London exhibitons. Of particular interest are the reviews of the 1924 exhibition in *The New Statesman* and the 1927 exhibition in *Apollo*.

The Plates: a Fantasy Portfolio

From an Ultimate Dim Thule III
(A record of Dreams) by S. H.
Sime

1 THE LITTLE GOD, THE MEDICINE MAN, AND THE BLUGGY BEESTE

The Sacrifice was completed, and the Star Dials were hinting of morn, as the rolling thunder on the Medicine Man's incomprehensible cabala, couched in somewhat dubious latinity, slackened into the weird wailing of the majestic formula of dismissal. Infernal filthy skirmishers hovered in hopes of a Lapsus Whatits-Name. But the little God only chortled, and something rumbled, and there was a kind of belching noise, and the Bluggy Beeste materialised. The Medicine Man was hoisted, shrieking, 'Oh, had I but served my Thing-um-a-jig as I have served my Tiddle-a-winx . . .' He was gone.

I said to myself, 'He's read that in a book', as I dived plumb into the Astral Plane.

Published in the *Idler*, August 1897

2 DREAMS, IDLE DREAMS

Deep in the recesses of that lonely wood stands the sacrificial altar. Whether another crime was added to the Wazir's list, or whether the Ordained One conquered the Event, I know not; for darkness fell as a pall, and the night became dreamless . . .

Published in the *Sketch*, May 1897

From an Ultimate Dim Thule I
(A record of Dreams) by S. H. Sime

3 THE QUEST OF THE OOF-BIRD

Away down the Valley of the Bho-Jees, over the Mountains of the Shadder-Jax, through the vast attenuated Limbo of The Cree-Pee, spat upon by the Ah-Ach-Sper, ensorcelled for countless aeons by the wiles of the Pewking Peout, clutched at and pinched by the Hootsmonarvgotye, chased by the Pit-a-Pats, and worried by the Gobble-Grob – away we quested in search of the nest of the Oof-Bird. Material objects should not be looked for in the Realms of Abstraction. We were cornered by the Aingnoos at last and dodged zealously back over the borders and through the Gates of Horn.

Published in the *Idler*, September 1897

4 THE INCUBUS

Published in the *Butterfly*, July 1899
Reprinted in the *Idler*, November 1900 and the *Magazine of Art*, in colour, April 1904

5 ON DESPERATE SEAS
Published in the *Butterfly*, April
1899
Reprinted in the *Idler*, June 1900

6 THE GATE OF KNOWLEDGE
Published in the *Pall Mall Magazine*, June 1905

7 THE NUNK
From *Bogey Beasts*. Pictures and verses by S. H. Sime. Music
by Josef Holbrooke. Goodwin and Tabb 1923

8 THE PST

From *Bogey Beasts*. Pictures and verses by S. H. Sime. Music
by Josef Holbrooke. Goodwin and Tabb 1923

9 THE PRAPSNOT
From *Bogey Beasts*. Pictures and verses by S. H. Sime. Music
by Josef Holbrooke. Goodwin and Tabb 1923

10 THE TWO-TAILED SOGG
From *Bogey Beasts*. Pictures and verses by S. H. Sime. Music
by Josef Holbrooke. Goodwin and Tabb 1923

11 THE FANTASY OF LIFE

The sudden discovery of that infamous den, that renowned and impregnable stronghold, the fear and envy of universal wizardry, not only drowned my memory of the quest – it involved me in perilous side issues. The malevolence underlying the Pophoffs' hospitable greeting passed unheeded by me, absorbed as I was, for how long I know not, in a profound and fatal curiosity.

'Drawing to Unknown Tales'.
Published in the *Tatler*, August 1901

12 A STORYETTE

'I can manage the ascent,' said I, 'but I will trouble you to call off your dog.' 'Sst!' whispered the wazir grinning, 'a pure-blooded armadiddle; speak him fair.' Anxious to get the ransom to his eminence without further delays I landed, remembering only after quitting the barque the warning of the ancient bird.

Published in the *Tatler*, January 1905

13 PEGANA

Frontispiece for *The Gods of Pegana* by Lord Dunsany
Elkin Mathews 1905

14 HISH

And when it is dark, all in the hour of Triboogie, Hish creepeth from the forest, the Lord of Silence, whose children are the bats, that have broken the command of their father, but in a voice that is ever so low, Hish husheth the mouse and all the whispers in the night; he maketh all noises still.

Illustration for *The Gods of Pegana* by Lord Dunsany
Elkin Mathews 1905

15 RĀNORĀDA

In the midst of the last of the deserts that are beyond Bodraháhn, in the centre of the Desert of Deserts, standeth the image that hath been hewn of old out of the living hill whose name is Rānorāda – the eye in the waste.

Illustration for *The Gods of Pegana* by Lord Dunsany
Elkin Mathews 1905

16 THE DREAMS OF MĀNA-YOOD-SUSHAĪ

When MĀNA-YOOD-SUSHAĪ had made the gods and Skarl, Skarl made a drum, and began to beat upon it that he might drum for ever. Then because he was weary after the making of the gods, and because of the drumming of Skarl, did MĀNA-YOOD-SUSHAĪ grow drowsy and fall asleep.

Illustration for *The Gods of Pegana* by Lord Dunsany
Elkin Mathews 1905

17 SLID

And Slid said: 'I am the Lord of gliding waters and of foaming waters and of still. I am the Lord of all the waters in the world and all that long streams garner in the hills; but the soul of Slid is in the Sea.'

Illustration for *The Gods of Pegana* by Lord Dunsany
Elkin Mathews 1905

18 MUNG AND THE BEAST OF MUNG

Then Mung went down into a waste of Afrik, and came upon the drought Umbool as he sat in the desert upon iron rocks, clawing with miserly grasp at the bones of men and breathing hot.

Illustration for *The Gods of Pegana* by Lord Dunsany
Elkin Mathews 1905

19 LO! THE GODS
For there the gods sat, each on a marble hill, each sitting with an elbow on his knee, and his chin upon his hand, and all the gods were smiling about Their lips.

Illustration for *Time and The Gods* by Lord Dunsany
Heinemann 1906

20 THE DIRGE OF SHIMONO KANI
Only Shimono Kani, the youngest of the gods, made him a harp out of the heart strings of all the elder gods, and, sitting upon the Path of Stars all in the Midst of Things, played upon the harp a dirge for the gods of Old.

Illustration for *Time and The Gods* by Lord Dunsany
Heinemann 1906

21 HOW SHAUN FOUND THE ULTIMATE GOD

All the next day Shaun toiled on to see Their faces by
starlight, but ere the night came up or one star shone, at set
of sun, Shaun fell down before the feet of his four gods. The
stars came out, and the faces of the four shone bright and
clear, but Shaun saw them not . . .

Illustration for *Time and The Gods* by Lord Dunsany
Heinemann 1906

22 INZANA CALLS UP THE THUNDER

When Inzana saw the Eclipse bearing her plaything away
she cried aloud to the thunder, who burst from Pegana and
fell howling upon the throat of the Eclipse, who dropped the
golden ball and let it fall towards earth.

Illustration for *Time and The Gods* by Lord Dunsany
Heinemann 1906

23 KAI LAUGHED

Then said the King, 'I pray to thee, who wilt take no gifts borne upon elephants or camels, to give me of thy mercy one second back, one grain of dust that clings to that hour in the heap that lies within thy cave.'

And at the word mercy, Kai laughed.

Illustration for *Time and The Gods* by Lord Dunsany Heinemann 1906

24 THE TOMB OF MORNING ZAI

And the gods came to a great sepulchre of onyx that stood upon four fluted pillars of white marble, each carved out of four mountains, and therein the gods laid Morning Zai because the old faith was fallen.

Illustration for *Time and The Gods* by Lord Dunsany Heinemann 1906

25 DEPARTURE OF HOTHRUN DATH

So about the dawn, Hothrun Dath crept away, fearing still
to hear behind him the breathing of the Famine, and set out
upon his journey whither pointed the graves of men.

Illustration for *Time and The Gods* by Lord Dunsany
Heinemann 1906

26 YAZUN IS GOD

Then on the altar of Zungari a priest had set a figure squat,
carven in purple agate, saying, 'Yazun is God'. Still the
gods sat and smiled.

Illustration for *Time and The Gods* by Lord Dunsany
Heinemann 1906

27 PATTERING LEAVES DANCED
Illustration for *Time and The Gods* by Lord Dunsany
Heinemann 1906

62

28 'EVEN I TOO! EVEN I TOO!'
There he alights from his palan-
quin and goes up to a throne of
ivory set in the garden's midst,
facing full westward, and sits
there alone, long regarding the
sunlight until it is gone. At this
hour trouble comes into the face
of Nehemoth. Men have heard
him muttering at the time of
sunset: 'Even I too! Even I too!'

Illustration for *The Sword of
Welleran* by Lord Dunsany
George Allen 1908

29 ONELEIGH

Now Oneleigh stands in a wide isolation, in the midst of a dark gathering of old whispering cedars. They nod their heads together when the North Wind comes, and nod again and agree, and furtively grow still again, and say no more awhile.

Illustration for *The Sword of Welleran* by Lord Dunsany George Allen 1908

30 TOM O'THE ROADS

To and fro, to and fro in the winds swung the bones and the soul of Tom, for the sins that he had sinned on the King's highway against the laws of the King; and with shadows and a lantern through the darkness, at the peril of their lives, came the three friends that his soul had won before it swung in chains.

Illustration for *The Sword of Welleran* by Lord Dunsany George Allen 1908. (First published in the *Idler*, December 1899.)

31 THE LIGHT OF ONG ZWARBA

Unadorned all save one, the Princess Linderith, who weareth Ong Zwarba and the three lesser gems of the sea. Such a stone is Ong Zwarba that there are none like it even in the turban of Nehemoth nor in all the sanctuaries of the sea.

Illustration for *The Sword of Welleran* by Lord Dunsany
George Allen 1908

32 A HERD OF BLACK CREATURES

Suddenly a herd of black creatures larger than blood-hounds came galloping in; they had large pendulous ears, their noses were to the ground sniffing, they went up to the lords and ladies of long ago and fawned about them disgustingly.

Illustration for *The Sword of Welleran* by Lord Dunsany
George Allen 1908

33 THE SOUL OF LA TRAVIATA

But into a great pink flower that was horrible and lovely
grew the soul of La Traviata; and it had in it two eyes but no
eyelids, and it stared constantly into the faces of all the
passers-by that went along the dusty road to Hell.

Illustration for *The Sword of Welleran* by Lord Dunsany
George Allen 1908

34 'GOOD-BYE!'

Illustration for *The Sword of Welleran* by Lord Dunsany
George Allen 1908

35 WE WOULD GALLOP
THROUGH AFRICA
Illustration for *A Dreamer's Tales*
by Lord Dunsany
George Allen 1910

36 ROMANCE COMES DOWN
OUT OF HILLY WOODLANDS
And when the light of some little
distant city makes a slight flush
upon the edge of the sky, and the
happy golden windows of the
homesteads stare gleaming into
the dark, then the old and holy
figure of Romance, cloaked even
to the face, comes down out of
hilly woodlands and bids dark
shadows to rise up and dance,
and sends the forest creatures
forth to prowl . . .

Illustration for *A Dreamer's Tales*
by Lord Dunsany
George Allen 1910

37 THE TERRIBLE MUD
'They took me down a stairway that was green with slimy
things and so came slowly to the terrible mud. There, in the
territory of forsaken things, they dug a shallow grave.
When they had finished they laid me in the grave . . .'

Illustration for *A Dreamer's Tales* by Lord Dunsany
George Allen 1910

38 BIRD OF THE RIVER
Illustration for *A Dreamer's Tales* by Lord Dunsany
George Allen 1910

39 THE SILENCE OF GED

He came back by night, and the next morning when the
tribe awoke they saw something that was like a man and yet
was not a man. And it sat on the hill with its elbows pointing
outwards and was quite still.

Illustration for *A Dreamer's Tales* by Lord Dunsany
George Allen 1910

40 THUBA MLEEN

And then I followed the Emperor's rapt glance, and I saw
the sailor lying on the floor, alive but hideously rent, and
the royal torturers were at work all around him. They had
torn long strips from him, but had not detached them, and
they were torturing the ends of them far away from the
sailor.

Illustration for *A Dreamer's Tales* by Lord Dunsany
George Allen 1910

41 THE EDGE OF THE WORLD
They came in silence to the foot of the stairs; and then it befell them as they drew near safety, in the night's most secret hour, some hand in an upper chamber lit a shocking light, lit it and made no sound.

Frontispiece for *The Book of Wonder* by Lord Dunsany
Heinemann 1912

42 THE OMINOUS COUGH
He was all but come to the end of the narrow way, when the woman listlessly uttered that ominous cough. The cough was too full of meaning to be disregarded. Thangobrind turned round and saw at once what he feared. The spider-idol had not stayed at home. The jeweller put his diamond gently upon the ground and drew his sword called Mouse.

Illustration for *The Book of Wonder* by Lord Dunsany
Heinemann 1912

43 THE HOUSE OF THE SPHINX

When I came to the House of the Sphinx it was already
dark. They made me eagerly welcome. And I, in spite of the
deed, was glad of any shelter from that ominous wood. I saw
at once that there had been a deed, although a cloak did all
that a cloak may do to conceal it.

The Sphinx was moody and silent.

Illustration for *The Book of Wonder* by Lord Dunsany
Heinemann 1912

44 I WISH I KNEW MORE ABOUT THE WAYS OF QUEENS

And almost Captain Shard and the Queen of the South
lived happily ever after, though still at evening those on
watch in the trees would see their captain sit with a puzzled
air or hear him muttering now and again in a discontented
way, 'I wish I knew more about the ways of Queens.'

Illustration for *The Book of Wonder* by Lord Dunsany
Heinemann 1912

45 ZRETAZOOLA

And suddenly there at his hooves in the dark of the plain appeared the cleft in the legendary lands, and Zretazoola sheltering in the cleft, and sunning herself in the evening . . . Three blasts he gave as he went upon that silver horn that is the world-old treasure of the centaurs. These were his wedding bells.

Illustration for *The Book of Wonder* by Lord Dunsany Heinemann 1912

46 HE FELT AS A MORSEL!

He sang of the malignity of time. Two tears welled in the eyes of the Gladsome Beast. Ackronnion moved the agate bowl to a suitable spot with his foot. He sang of autumn and of passing away. Then the Beast wept as the frore hills weep in the thaw, and the tears splashed big into the agate bowl . . . The bowl was full. Ackronnion was desperate: the Beast was so close. Once he thought that its mouth was watering! – but it was only the tears that had run on the lips of the Beast. He felt as a morsel! The Beast was ceasing to weep!

Illustration for *The Book of Wonder* by Lord Dunsany Heinemann 1912

47 THE LEAN HIGH HOUSE OF THE GNOLES

But the gnoles had watched him through knavish holes that they bore in trunks of the trees and the unearthly silence gave way, as it were with a grace, to the rapid screams of Tonker as they picked him up from behind – screams that came faster and faster until they were incoherent. And where they took him it is not good to ask, and what they did with him I shall not say.

Illustration for *The Book of Wonder* by Lord Dunsany
Heinemann 1912

48 THERE THE GIBBELINS LIVED AND DISCREDITABLY FED

The Gibbelins eat, as is well known, nothing less good than man . . .

Their tower stands on the other side of that river known to Homer – *Ὠ ῥόος ὠ'χεανοίο* as he called it – which surrounds the world. And where the river is narrow and fordable the tower was built by the Gibbelins' gluttonous sires, for they liked to see burglars rowing easily to their steps.

Illustration for *The Book of Wonder* by Lord Dunsany
Heinemann 1912

49 THE CITY OF NEVER

But when they came to the heights that venturous rider saw huge and fair to the left of him the destined City of Never, and he beheld the towers of Lel and Lek, Neerib and Akathooma, and the cliffs of Toldenarba a-glistering in the twilight like an alabaster statue of the Evening.

Illustration for *The Book of Wonder* by Lord Dunsany Heinemann 1912

50 THE CORONATION OF MR THOMAS SHAP

A fountain hurled up, clattering, ceaselessly into the air armfuls on armfuls of diamonds, a deep hush waited for the golden trumpets, the holy coronation night was come. At the top of those old, worn steps, going down we know not whither, stood the king in the emerald-and-amethyst cloak, the ancient garb of the Thuls; beside him lay that Sphinx that for the last few weeks had advised him in his affairs.

Illustration for *The Book of Wonder* by Lord Dunsany Heinemann 1912

51 THE BAD OLD WOMAN IN BLACK

The bad old woman in black ran down the street of the ox-butchers.

Windows at once were opened high up in those crazy gables; heads were thrust out: it was she.

Frontispiece for *Tales of Wonder* by Lord Dunsany
Elkin Mathews 1916

52 THE BIRD OF THE DIF-FICULT EYE

And there on a lower branch within easy reach he clearly saw the Bird of the Difficult Eye sitting upon the nest for which she is famous. Her face was towards those three inscrutable mountains, far-off on the other side of the risky seas, whose hidden valleys are fairyland.

Illustration for *Tales of Wonder* by Lord Dunsany
Elkin Mathews 1916

53 THE LONG PORTER'S TALE

Not even fabulous beasts were near him now nor strange
demoniac trees, nothing but the snow and the clean bare
crag above it on which was Tong Tong Tarrup.

Illustration for *Tales of Wonder* by Lord Dunsany
Elkin Mathews 1916

54 THE SECRET OF THE SEA

Midnight and Moonlight and the Temple in the Sea. Bill
Smiles clearly remembers, and all the derelicts in the world
were there, the old abandoned ships. The figureheads were
nodding to themselves and blinking at the image. The
image was a woman of white marble on a pedestal . . .

Illustration for *Tales of Wonder* by Lord Dunsany
Elkin Mathews 1916

55 HOW ALI CAME TO THE BLACK COUNTRY

Guided by Ali all three set forth for the Midlands. And by
the reverence that was manifest in the faces of Shep and
Shooshan towards the person of Ali, some knew what Ali
carried, while others said it was the tablets of the Law,
others the name of God, and others that he must have a lot
of money about him.

Illustration for *Tales of Wonder* by Lord Dunsany
Elkin Mathews 1916

56 THE LOOT OF LOMA

It was Laughing Face who said it and who gathered thirty
braves and led them into Loma with their tomahawks and
their bows; there were only four left now, but they had the
loot of Loma on a mule.

Illustration for *Tales of Wonder* by Lord Dunsany
Elkin Mathews 1916

57 THE HUNTING OF THE UNICORN

No moments passed before many another hound leaped on to the unicorn, each with a chosen grip, for all that they looked like a rabble rolling and heaving by chance. Orion thrust no more, for many hounds all at once were between him and his enemy's throat. Awful groans came from the unicorn, such sounds as are not heard in the fields we know . . .

Frontispiece for *The King of Elfland's Daughter* by Lord Dunsany
Heinemann 1924

58 WHEN WE HAD HUNTED THE MOON ENOUGH WE CAME BACK THROUGH THE WOOD

Frontispiece for *My Talks with Dean Spanley* by Lord Dunsany
Heinemann 1936

Index

Numbers in italics refer to pages on which illustrations occur.
Plate numbers refer to illustrations in the *Fantasy Portfolio*.